The Thinking Game

ALSO BY KARA LANE

The Thinking Game

A Winning Strategy for Achieving Your Goals

Kara Lane

Kara Lane Publishing
Carmel

www.karalane.com

Library of Congress Control Number: 2019904294

Hardcover ISBN 978-1-7339379-2-4
Paperback ISBN 978-1-7339379-0-0
Ebook ISBN 978-1-7339379-1-7

Printed in the United States of America

First Edition

Contents

"The book to read is not the one that thinks for you, but the one that makes you think."

—attributed to Harper Lee (and James McCosh)

A Note on Quotes

The Thinking Game is a strategic guide on how to think better so you can achieve more of your goals. Where I have included quotes, it is because I read something about thinking that made an important point and expressed it well. The quotations indicate it didn't come from me. The problem is that it isn't always clear who the quotes did come from originally. How do you prove who first came up with a quote in its current form?

As quote investigator Garson O'Toole points out in his book, *Hemingway Didn't Say That*, many quotes are misattributed. Once misquotes occur, they rapidly spread online and in print. One reason misattribution occurs is that someone famous repeats something they heard or read and from then on the famous person is given credit for the quote. Another reason is that we remember a quote but not who said it. If it's witty, we think it may have been Mark Twain. If it's intelligent, we think it may have been Albert Einstein. Even the oft-quoted and misquoted Yogi Berra said, "I really didn't say everything I said." Yet another reason for misquotes is that someone makes a great point, but someone else paraphrases what they said to make it quotable. For instance, "No one can make you feel inferior without your consent" is usually attributed to Eleanor Roosevelt. What she actually said, as reported in the newspapers at the time, was "A snub is the effort of a person who feels superior to make someone else feel inferior. To do so, he has to find someone who can be made to feel inferior." So do you attribute the catchier quote to Eleanor or to her unknown paraphraser?

This is a book about thinking, which includes solving problems. So this is how I've solved the quote-verification problem: I have attributed each quote to whomever it is commonly attributed to, but I have also given credit parenthetically to other credible sources if I could readily identify them. Thinking should be goal-based. I assume that your goal for reading *The Thinking Game* is to become a more effective thinker, not to become an expert on the origin of quotes...feel free to quote me on that.

Introduction:

Why Play *The Thinking Game*?

"Watch your thoughts; they become words. Watch your words; they become actions. Watch your actions; they become habits. Watch your habits; they become character. Watch your character; it becomes your destiny."

—attributed to Lao Tzu (and Frank Outlaw)

What would you be without the ability to think? A body? Your body keeps you alive, but you experience life through your mind. How you perceive yourself, other people, and the world is determined by your thinking. How you think affects how you feel, what you say, and what you do. Thinking drives your actions, and your actions drive your outcomes. Everything begins in the mind.

The quality of your thinking determines your level of success and satisfaction. Success is the ability to achieve the goals that you have chosen. Satisfaction is a feeling of well-being that comes from being happy with yourself and your life. Some people achieve one or the other, some both, some neither. Your thought process is the key to achieving both success and satisfaction. To live better, you must think better.

Ah, but there's the rub. How do you think better? For starters, it helps to understand how the mind works. There are many layers to the mind, but let's keep it simple and divide it into two parts: the conscious mind and the unconscious mind (a.k.a. the subconscious mind). Your conscious mind includes everything you're aware of, including what you're currently thinking, feeling, and perceiving. It also includes whatever thoughts you can bring into consciousness from memory. Your unconscious mind includes everything else that exists in your mind but is outside your awareness. It includes hidden beliefs, biases, feelings, memories, and habits formed in the past that still influence your thoughts, experiences, and behavior in the present. You need to understand your conscious mind because that is what you can control. You need to understand your unconscious mind because that is what will otherwise control you.

Much of what is now unconscious was once conscious. A lifetime of thoughts and perceptions have passed from your conscious to your unconscious, shaping who you are and how you automatically think and behave today. You cannot directly access your unconscious mind, but by changing your conscious thought process (how you think), you can improve your unconscious thought content (what you think). That is how you upgrade your thinking.

Through conscious thought, you can set and achieve meaningful goals, solve challenging problems, and make better decisions. Conscious thinking helps you figure out what you want and gives you the power to get it. You are not a pawn of other people, your past experiences, or your current circumstances. You can become the queen or king of your own life if you put on your thinking crown.

Anyone can learn to think better with the right mindset, skills, and techniques. The problem is that most people don't think they need to improve their thinking, or that it's even possible. To them, thinking is like breathing. It just happens. They believe that how they think is no more subject to change than the color of their eyes. As a result, they default to unconscious thinking, which is automatic and effortless. And unfortunately, it's also frequently wrong.

If you stop to think about it, you know that just because you have a thought doesn't make it true. That would imply your thinking was 100 percent accurate, 100 percent of the time. Ridiculous, right? But even if we concede that our thoughts have sometimes been wrong *in the past*, we continue to believe that what we are thinking *right this minute* is true. I think; therefore I am right. Of course, anyone who disagrees with us thinks they are the one who is right, which is why relationship issues arise.

Besides causing issues with other people, faulty thinking can harm you in other ways. If you are not thinking clearly and rationally, you will not be able to figure out the best solutions to problems. You may make bad decisions or procrastinate on making any decision at all. If emotions cloud your judgment, you may blame your unsatisfactory results on other people or bad luck. By doing so, you won't learn anything from the situation that could help you succeed in the future. Flawed thinking may also create self-doubt, causing you to avoid pursuing challenging goals that you are capable of achieving. When that happens, you limit your potential due to a lack of confidence, not a lack of competence.

If you don't continue to stimulate your mind, you will end up living in your mental comfort zone, also known as the no-risk, no-reward zone. You may feel safer there, but you risk becoming stuck in a boring life that is too small for you. As business magnate Steve Jobs said, "Your thoughts construct patterns like scaffolding in your mind. You are really etching chemical patterns. In most cases, people get stuck in those patterns, just like grooves in a record, and they never get out of them." To get out of a rut requires different thinking than what got you into it.

People who are willing to work on improving their thinking skills have a big advantage over everyone else. Because thinking affects every area of life, conscious thinkers achieve higher levels of success. Some people are born smart and have a natural talent for thinking. But just like a natural athlete who fails to develop their talent, a smart person who fails to develop their thinking can be surpassed by those willing to work harder to improve their skills.

The Thinking Game

Conscious thought takes effort. Fortunately, thinking more effectively gets easier with practice and the right techniques.

Perhaps more people would consciously think about their thought process if they considered how critical it is to a satisfying life. Thinking is at the root of everything. Some people will argue that how we feel is more important than how we think, but you cannot separate the two. A feeling of gratitude arises when you think about the things for which you are grateful. A feeling of worry arises when you think about what could go wrong. A feeling of anger arises when you think someone has wronged you. Thoughts drive feelings. If you change your thinking, your feelings will follow.

Your thinking affects your words, which affect your relationships. If you have ever wished you could take back something you said, you know the power of words. Words are like weapons; they wound sometimes. We cannot unsay what has been said. Many personal and business relationships have been ruined by a failure to think before speaking. Fortunately, the right words can also save a relationship.

Your thinking drives your actions, which drive your results. As philosopher James Allen said, "All that you accomplish or fail to accomplish with your life is the direct result of your thoughts." Action may not always follow thinking but thinking always precedes action. Unfortunately, much of our thinking is unconscious and habitual. Dr. Deepak Chopra notes that we have an estimated 60,000 to 80,000 thoughts a day, but most of them are repetitive. If our thoughts are the same, our behavior will be the same, and our results will be the same – day after day, year after year. If you want different results, start with different thoughts.

You can consciously think about the direction you want your personal and work life to take. Unlike the demoralized majority who hope other people, circumstances, or their luck will change, you can bring about changes yourself. By combining conscious thought with definite action, you can get what you want and need. Intentional thinking gives you greater control, freedom, and confidence.

The rewards of better thinking are clear, so how can we motivate ourselves to think more intentionally and effectively?

We can approach thinking like a game: *The Thinking Game.*

Think about the kind of games you play: board games, card games, video games, casino games, sports games, etc. What do all games have in common? A game is an activity defined by rules that you win by using skill, knowledge, and luck. Thinking is also an activity defined by rules that you win by using skill, knowledge, and luck.

If you approach thinking as if it were a game, you will begin to see problems as obstacles to overcome in order to win the prize. The prize is the achievement of your goal or purpose. When you play a game, you expect challenges. It would be a pretty boring game if there weren't any. So why do we get so frustrated about challenges in life? They're all just part of the game. The more challenging the problem, the more satisfying it will be when you solve it. And you will be able to solve it if you use the principles and techniques you'll find in *The Thinking Game*.

Additionally, part of the fun of playing a game is not knowing how it will turn out. You win some; you lose some. An even better philosophy from *The Thinking Game* is you win some; you learn some. If you develop a thinking mindset and use the skills we'll discuss, you will win more often as you pursue your goals. But you can't win them all. When you fall short of achieving a goal, learn from the experience. Analyze your results and refine your strategy using the tools we'll talk about in the following chapters. Don't give up when things don't work out. If at first you don't succeed, think, think again.

Thinking is a strategy game in which you set a goal and decide how best to achieve it. *The Thinking Game* will provide you with the rules, the tools, and the strategies you need to think more effectively. You will learn how to set the right goal, create the right plan, take the right action, and analyze and improve your results. You will better understand yourself, other people, and situations. You will gain greater control over your thoughts, feelings, and behavior. You will be able to predict the consequences of your actions, leading to improved decision-making. You will be able to define success for yourself and then figure out ways to achieve it.

Here's a quick rundown of what you'll find in *The Thinking Game*:

Part One helps you understand the rules and realities that govern thinking.

Chapter 1 covers *The Thinking Game* rules. The object of the game is to achieve a goal or purpose that you have chosen. The seven rules that govern how you play the game are the rules of reality. You are free to play the game however you want but ignoring reality won't change it. You'll achieve greater success and satisfaction if you accept reality and work with it instead of against it.

Chapter 2 explores the unconscious mind and how it differs from the conscious mind. You'll gain a greater understanding of how your unconscious beliefs, biases, and feelings can control your life unless you learn to manage them. With this knowledge comes power. You'll be able to play defense to keep your unconscious mind from interfering with your conscious goals. Everyone knows defense wins championships.

Part Two provides guidance on how to improve conscious thinking.

Chapter 3 kicks things off with a discussion of the six personality traits that comprise the thinking mindset. These traits are common among the world's greatest thinkers. By acquiring traits like curiosity and persistence, you'll find it easier and more enjoyable to improve your thinking. This chapter also provides challenges to help you further develop each trait.

Chapter 4 identifies four core critical thinking skills and provides tips on how to strengthen each one. You get better at thinking skills through deliberate practice. The more you analyze, the better you become at analysis. The more you organize, the better you become at organization...and so on. Improving your thinking skills will allow you to get more done, in less time, with better results.

Chapter 5 outlines twelve effective thinking techniques, which are tools to prompt better critical and creative thinking. Critical thinking is logic-based. Checklists and the 5 Whys are examples of critical thinking techniques. Creative thinking is imagination-based. Meditation and Mind Mapping are examples of creative thinking techniques.

Chapter 6 wraps up Part Two with a list of questions to trigger your thinking in the major areas of your life, such as your relationships, money, and health. Asking and answering questions is fundamental to effective thinking. By asking and answering the *right* questions, you will become a confident, decisive, and clear thinker. As your thinking continues to improve, so will your results.

While Part Two covers how to improve conscious thinking, Part Three covers how to apply conscious thinking to the achievement of goals by following a 4-step process.

Chapter 7 discusses the first step, which is setting the right goal. By focusing on criteria such as clarity and measurability, you can accurately define what you want to happen. The information provided will help you set the appropriate goal for achieving a result, changing a habit, solving a problem, or making a decision.

Chapter 8 covers the second step, which is creating the right plan of action. A goal without a definite plan is just wishful thinking. Unlike the cartoon that solves a difficult problem by inserting "and then a miracle occurs" near the end, you must carefully think through the specific steps of your plan. This chapter provides a simple step-by-step process for creating an action plan.

Chapter 9 goes over the third step, which is taking the right action to achieve your goal. Many things can derail a plan: other people, bad luck, and your own actions – or lack of action. This chapter provides strategies for taking effective action to execute your plan and for knowing when to diverge from the plan.

Chapter 10 discusses the final step in goal achievement, which is to evaluate your results. Less successful people do not spend much time on this step. Either they achieved the goal, or they didn't – end of story. But it is not the end of the story for successful people. They analyze the outcome, regardless of whether they succeeded or failed, and use what they learn to improve their future results. If you create after-action reports as suggested in this chapter, you will achieve your goals more quickly.

The Thinking Game

I wrote *The Thinking Game* because I love thinking and using analysis to understand the world. I always considered myself an effective thinker because I graduated from college with Highest Distinction, became a Certified Public Accountant (CPA) after receiving the High-Grade Award for Indiana when I passed the CPA exam, and became the Vice President of Financial Planning for an insurance company in my thirties. However, when I left the corporate world to work for myself, I realized there were chinks in my thinking armor. I excelled in structured environments where professors and employers set the goals and my job was to figure out how best to achieve them. But out on my own, I realized that while my research, analysis, and organizational skills were well honed, I needed to strengthen other thinking skills, such as decision-making. As I continued to study the mind, I discovered that effective thinkers not only consciously develop their critical and creative thinking skills, but they also learn how to harness the power of their unconscious minds. My goal in writing *The Thinking Game* is to help you become a more effective thinker so you can set and achieve the goals that are most important to you.

Playing *The Thinking Game* will help you set the right goals, create the right plans, and take the right action to get the results you want. If you enjoy thinking, you will intentionally do it more often. If you do it more often, you will get better at it. If you get better at it, you will reap the rewards of conscious thinking in the form of better outcomes, personally and professionally.

The object of *The Thinking Game* is to achieve a goal or purpose that you have chosen. You can play the game over and over again with different goals.

Let the game begin…

Part One:

Understanding the Rules and

Realities of Thinking

Chapter 1:

The Thinking Game Rules

"If you don't deal with reality, then reality will deal with you."

—attributed to Alex Haley

Like any other game, *The Thinking Game* has rules that govern how the game is played. Games that have stood the test of time have very few rules but an endless number of winning strategies. Think of games like chess, poker, or Go. You can learn the rules quickly, but it can take a lifetime to master the game. Thinking has been around longer than any game, and it too can be played with just a short list of rules.

The rules that govern *The Thinking Game* are deceptively simple, so most people won't fully grasp their power. The rules are easy to understand but are sometimes hard to follow. The rules reflect reality, which – judging by the popularity of virtual reality games – many people prefer to escape. But thinking takes place in the real world, and the actions that stem from our thinking have real-world consequences. Successful players work with reality rather than fighting against it. Understanding and applying the rules leads to success and satisfaction. Ignoring the rules leads to failure and frustration.

Rule #1: The object of *The Thinking Game* is to achieve a goal

The highest and best use of thinking is to aim it at a specific goal or purpose. Mind chatter is not thinking. We tend to believe that anything that goes on in our heads is thinking, but many times we're just regurgitating old thoughts. Repetitive thoughts keep us stuck where we are; old thoughts can't take us to new places. Conscious thinking is intentional. It leads somewhere. You win *The Thinking Game* by setting and achieving a goal.

The goal itself can be anything you choose. It can be an achievement goal, such as writing a book, getting a promotion, or running a marathon. It can be a habit goal, such as exercising daily, eating healthier, or giving up cigarettes. It can be a problem-solving goal, such as resolving an issue with a family member or figuring out why a competitor is suddenly outperforming you. It can be a decision-making goal, like deciding where to live, work, or attend school. The goal can be any result you desire.

In addition to applying Rule #1 to major goals, the rule can be used to upgrade your everyday thought process. The way we think about anything tends to become the way we think about everything. For instance, some people's thoughts automatically jump to the negative. They may be worriers. They may be overly critical of others. They may constantly complain about their circumstances. If you notice yourself dwelling on negative thoughts, ask yourself: What's the point of this line of thinking?

Pay attention to repetitive thoughts that are not productive. Such thoughts disturb your peace of mind and don't change anything. For instance, I would find myself thinking "that's not fair" when someone appeared to have an unfair advantage or said or did something unkind. Then one day I came across this quote on the blog of author John Spence: "If you expect the world to be fair with you because you are fair, you're fooling yourself. That's like expecting the lion not to eat you because you didn't eat him." Funny, and a good point. Believing reality should be something different than it is serves no useful purpose. You can act to change your reality, but you first have to accept that it is what it currently is.

If you find yourself dwelling on the same issues over and over, acknowledge your thoughts and feelings but then think about what you want to do about the situation. What's the goal? Do you want to accept the situation, or change it? Do you want to improve the relationship, or leave it? Is there a real issue, or are you making a big deal out of nothing? You get your thinking back on track by pointing it in a more productive direction. Put yourself back in control by focusing on the immediate goal. Think about what you want to happen and then how you can make it happen.

By regularly engaging in intentional, goal-based thinking, you'll be ahead of the game compared to most people. As playwright George Bernard Shaw quipped, "Few people think more than two or three times a year. I have made an international reputation for myself thinking once or twice a week." That's a start.

Rule #2: You play the game with others but only control your own moves

The Thinking Game is a multiplayer game. Other players affect your thoughts, feelings, and actions, and you affect theirs. They act, and you react. You act, and they react. You may be able to influence other people, but you only control your own moves, not theirs. They have their own goals, which won't always align with yours. You are not a pawn in their game, nor are they a pawn in yours.

Trying to control other people wastes your time and causes unnecessary suffering, but it's a temptation that's hard to resist. You want the freedom to think and do as you please, but you may not always grant that same freedom to others. Your life would be easier if everyone else agreed with your thinking and went along with what you wanted. We get annoyed when we think someone is trying to manipulate us but may not even notice when we are the ones doing the manipulating. Common forms of manipulation include using guilt, intimidation, criticism, flattery, pulling rank, playing helpless, and withholding affection.

The Thinking Game

The way we view the world is shaped by our beliefs, experiences, personalities, and interests, and we each grant privileged status to our own thoughts and feelings. I completely identify with what I think and feel, and you completely identify with what you think and feel. The key to relationships is mutual recognition, which acknowledges and respects that each of us perceives the world through our own unique perspective. We do not see things objectively. We are each at the center of our own universe encountering other people who are at the center of their universe. Philosopher Roger Scruton explains that in interacting with the *other* person, "I am forced to recognize that I too am *other* to the one who is *other* to me." If you truly understand that concept, it will change the nature of your relationships. You will still see things from your unique perspective, but you will also be able to appreciate the validity of other viewpoints. Their views are as real and important to them as yours are to you. You will not be bothered by what other people say or do. You will not take things personally because you will know that other people are just playing *their* game like you're playing *yours*.

Make it a habit to pause before responding to what others say and do. A wise saying inspired by Viktor Frankl's teaching (and paraphrased by Stephen Covey) is "Between stimulus and response, there is a space. In that space is our power to choose our response. In our response lies our growth and our freedom." When someone says or does something *to* you, wait to get your emotions in check before responding. You will then be able to think clearly instead of saying or doing something you may regret. It is also good advice for those times when someone asks something *of* you. If you take a minute to think before responding, you are more likely to make a good choice and less likely to be manipulated into a bad one. The most successful players of *The Thinking Game* accept the things they cannot control and control the things they can.

An easy way to remember Rule #2 is to think of it as a separation of duties. Your job is to exercise control over your thoughts, feelings, and actions. What other people choose to think, feel, and do is their job. That does not mean that what they do won't affect you. You may not be able to control them, but you can control what you do in light of their behavior. They can do the same with you.

Rule #3: You can play or pass but there are consequences to your actions

When playing *The Thinking Game*, you always have the option to play or pass. To play means to take action. To pass means to do nothing.

There are consequences to our actions, but we often fail to think about them. A major reason we may not make the connection between our current circumstances and our past actions is because of the delay between cause and effect.

The Thinking Game

If the results of our actions were immediately obvious, we would likely change what we do. If we instantly became overweight when we overate, we would consume less food. If we immediately became wealthy when we spent money wisely, we would be more mindful of our spending habits. If our relationships ended the minute we were critical or selfish, we would be kinder and more generous to the people in our lives. But consequences often come much later and are the result of cumulative actions, so we often fail to see the connection between our actions and our outcomes.

Another reason we fail to consider the consequences of our actions is that we get caught up in our emotions. If we stopped to think about it, we would realize that getting into a shouting match at work is probably not a good idea. But we're not thinking, we're feeling. We may regret our actions later, but by then it may be too late.

There are also consequences to inaction. Taking no action is often worse than taking the wrong action. If you do something that doesn't work out, you can learn from it. If you do nothing, there is nothing to learn, and no progress is made. Inaction often shows up as procrastination and indecision. Avoiding meaningful action can become a habit which keeps you from getting the results you want.

An effective way to think about Rule #3 is to consider Future You. Current You is largely driven by your unconscious mind, which only cares about today. What do you feel like doing right now? What do you want to avoid doing right now? Current You doesn't care about consequences, but Future You will. Remember that Current You was once Future You. Imagine how your life would be different now if you had made different choices in the past.

Make it a habit to consider the future consequences of actions you are thinking about taking (or avoiding) today. Current You will tend to choose what's easiest and feels good in the moment. But unless you want your future to mirror your present, you might want to think of Future You. Ask questions like, What is likely to happen if I do this? Will I regret it later if I don't do this? By consciously thinking about your future, you can make better decisions today and create a better life tomorrow.

Rule #4: Greater goals require greater time and effort

The motto of the Navy SEALs is "the only easy day was yesterday." The rest of us tend to prefer easy over effort. We want instant results, or we move on to something less demanding. We want things to come easily to us because hard things make us feel uncomfortable and incompetent. Hard things trigger inferiority complexes that originated in childhood when we were weak and adults seemed strong. But the only way to become competent is to stick with hard things until they become easy. That takes time and effort. In today's culture, it may be taboo to suggest hard work pays off, but it does. Sorry.

Even geniuses aren't exempt from this rule. When people called Michelangelo a genius, he said, "If you knew how much work went into it, you wouldn't call it genius." Mozart was a child prodigy who began composing at age five, but he would not have achieved much if he had stopped composing at age six. If even geniuses must put in the time and effort to achieve their goals, so must the rest of us.

Effort should be revered, not feared. The challenge is what makes things interesting. What fun would it be to play *The Thinking Game* if there were no challenges? Easy is boring. Anyone can do easy things, which is why doing them is not satisfying and doesn't build confidence. Effort makes you smarter, stronger, and more successful. You are more capable than you know, but you will not realize your potential unless you stretch beyond what is easy and familiar.

Don't get too hung up on how much time it will take to achieve a goal. Time and energy are limited in any given day, but if you add up the days, weeks, months, and years, your time and energy are practically unlimited. Regardless of your age or circumstances, you still have time to set and achieve your chosen goals.

If you're concerned about how much time and effort it will take to achieve your goal, consider what you would otherwise be doing. Do you have something better to do? There's a concept in finance called *opportunity cost*, which refers to the benefit you give up by choosing one alternative over another. When you're weighing your options, think about the opportunity cost of pursuing your goal. Is realizing your goal worth your time and effort? If not, choose a better goal.

If you're not willing to put in the time and effort to get what you want, you've got to ask yourself one question: How bad do you want it? Apparently, not bad enough.

Rule #5: Luck is a wild card which can work for you or against you

Luck is a factor in *The Thinking Game*, just like it is in any other game. Sometimes luck works in your favor, and sometimes it works against you. Everyone experiences both good luck and bad. It's how you respond to it that matters.

Optimistic people expect to experience good luck, so they watch for it. They quickly spot opportunities that others miss because they are paying attention. They seek, and they find. When they get lucky breaks, they appreciate them and make the most of them. Their belief that they are lucky becomes a self-fulfilling prophecy. Because they expect lucky breaks, they get them in spades.

Pessimists expect bad luck, and they are not disappointed. In poker, a *bad beat* is when the player who initially has the strongest hand ends up losing to a weaker starting hand. Some poker players get emotional after a bad beat and go *on tilt*, meaning they get frustrated and start playing irrationally. The same thing happens to people who consider themselves victims of bad luck. They feel sorry for themselves instead of shaking it off and refocusing on what they can control. Even when pessimists experience lucky breaks, they discount them or completely fail to notice them. Since they don't see their good luck, they can't take advantage of it.

You can prepare for good luck by consciously working on your goals while keeping your eyes open for lucky breaks. When you spot opportunities, act quickly and decisively to take advantage of them. You can defend yourself against bad luck by thinking about what could go wrong when you're making plans. Prepare a contingency plan and be ready to implement it if needed.

The smartest way to think about luck is that it affects your life but does not define it. There's no question that some people start life with the lucky break of being born into a favorable environment. If that was the case for you, make the most of your good fortune. If you were not so lucky, remember the old adage that it's not how you start, it's how you finish. You can't change your past environment, but you can change your future circumstances if you're willing to put in the time and effort to do it. Your success will be especially sweet because you'll know you earned it despite the odds stacked against you.

You don't control luck, so there's no point in counting on good luck or worrying about bad luck. Be grateful for good luck when it happens. Deal with bad luck when it happens. Then move on.

Rule #6: You will progress more quickly if you learn from your results

The most successful players in any game adjust their play based on their results. The worse players continue to play the game the same way every time and hope they get lucky. That same behavior explains why some people achieve their goals relatively quickly, and others never achieve them at all. As poet Charles Bukowski said, "A life can change in a tenth of a second or sometimes it can take 70 years." The winners of *The Thinking Game* learn from their results to speed things along.

If you're unhappy with an outcome, think about what might have caused it. If there's a problem, don't look to place blame or make excuses. Seek the truth about the situation so you can improve it. Understanding the current reality is the first step toward changing it.

If you're happy with an outcome, see what you can learn from it. If a project turned out particularly well or a relationship is going better than usual, think about the potential causes. Then build on your success now and in the future.

Results don't lie. Analyze your results to see what they tell you and then use what you learn. Notice what works and do more of that. Notice what doesn't work and do less of that. It's not complicated, but it takes time and effort to do your analysis. It's worth the time.

Instead of learning from their successes and failures, many people do stuff and then do more of the same stuff regardless of whether or not it's working. They make slow (or no) progress on their goals because they're not learning from their results. They're not improving their thinking. They're just mindlessly repeating the same actions and hoping for better results.

Using results as feedback to change what you do works because of the compound effect in which small changes accumulate over time to produce big results. You don't have to figure out the perfect solution; you just have to continue making adjustments to what you're doing until you get the results you want.

Rule #7: You win by mastering your conscious mind and managing your unconscious mind

According to some cognitive neuroscientists, we are only conscious of around 5 percent of our cognitive activity, and the other 95 percent of what drives our thoughts, emotions, and behavior is unconscious. If that doesn't boggle your mind, it should. Even if their numbers are off, it suggests that an overwhelming percentage of what goes on in our minds is unconscious. We cannot directly control our unconscious mind because it is outside our awareness, and yet it largely controls how we think, feel, and behave. The problem this poses is enormous. Fortunately, there is a simple solution.

First, the problem. Social psychologist Timothy Wilson noted that our brains could unconsciously process around 11 million pieces of information per second. It's amazing that our brains can efficiently handle so much information, control our bodily functions, *and* enable us to remember things. The problem is that what goes on in our cranium uses up to 20 percent of our body's energy. To conserve energy, the unconscious mind takes shortcuts. It looks for patterns, makes assumptions, and jumps to conclusions without slowing down for fact-checking. Like an overworked employee, it makes mistakes. Our unconscious minds sacrifice accuracy for speed.

It might not be so bad if our unconscious minds conducted periodic audits and purged inaccurate and outdated records. For instance, it would be nice if your mind would delete that nagging feeling of inferiority you picked up as a 3-year old munchkin because your 6-year old brother did everything better than you. But that's not how it works. That feeling of insecurity stayed with you and was reinforced whenever you encountered a similar situation that made you feel you were not good enough. Even if your expectations were unrealistic in situations where someone else was older or more experienced than you, the only thing your unconscious mind registered was that you came up short. If you're not aware that your feelings of inferiority are based on faulty beliefs, you may automatically respond in self-limiting or ineffective ways whenever those feelings are triggered.

An important part of *The Thinking Game* is taking time to identify and examine your thoughts and feelings. When you feel a strong emotion (such as inferiority), stop for a moment to consider why you're feeling it. Think back to the first time you remember feeling that way. Compare your current situation to the earlier one to see if they're comparable or if they differ in important ways. Ask yourself if what you're thinking is true or if it's just a habitual thought that arises in certain situations. Understanding the *why* behind an unconscious thought can help you manage the conscious thoughts and actions that result from it.

You obviously cannot take away the automatic aspect of your mind, nor would you want to. If you had to consciously think about everything all of the time, you would be exhausted. What you want to do is manage your unconscious mind. You want to update it with better information and train it to work for you instead of against you. So how do you do that?

The solution is to master your conscious mind and allow it to ingrain better beliefs and habits in your unconscious mind. You will learn how to do that in Parts Two and Three. What's important to note here is that when you improve your conscious thinking, you automatically improve your unconscious thinking. Your unconscious mind is trying to conserve energy, so it believes whatever your conscious mind feeds it. For example, in the past, if you would set goals but not follow through, your unconscious said, "Got it. You don't follow through." Your unconscious mind reminded you of that "fact" each time you set a new goal. Your past habit of quitting handicapped you from the outset. If you now begin to consciously think about what you want to achieve and then change your behavior by making yourself follow through, your unconscious mind will jump to a new and improved conclusion, "OK, got it. You follow through." Now when you decide to do something, your unconscious mind will produce a feeling of confidence that you will follow through. What used to be hard will become second nature. The more times you consciously set goals and persist until you achieve them, the more your unconscious mind will override the old information with the new. And that, in a nutshell, is how you train your unconscious mind.

Everyone plays some version of *The Thinking Game*, but many play it unconsciously and without understanding the rules. As a result, they fight reality and reality wins. They believe the solution to their problems is somewhere over the rainbow. They count on other people and the world to change so they won't have to. But *The Thinking Game* is played by the rules of the real world, not some fantasy world. You win the game by mastering your conscious mind and managing your unconscious mind.

To recap, these are the rules of *The Thinking Game*:

The Thinking Game

Rule #1: The object of *The Thinking Game* is to achieve a goal

Rule #2: You play the game with others but only control your own moves

Rule #3: You can play or pass but there are consequences to your actions

Rule #4: Greater goals require greater time and effort

Rule #5: Luck is a wild card which can work for you or against you

Rule #6: You will progress more quickly if you learn from your results

Rule #7: You win by mastering your conscious mind and managing your unconscious mind

The more you consciously play *The Thinking Game*, the better you will get at playing it. You'll win more often and achieve more of your goals. The game becomes easier the more you play it. And yet you can never completely master the game, so it continues to be interesting and challenging throughout your life – even as you move up to higher levels of play.

As you play *The Thinking Game*, keep in mind that each game is part of a larger game. The largest game of all is your life. Worth playing for? Then read on.

Chapter 2:

Managing Your Unconscious Mind

"Until you make the unconscious conscious, it will direct your life and you will call it fate."

—attributed to Carl Jung

Since your conscious mind is directly within your control, it may seem odd to focus on the unconscious mind first. Why not jump right to a discussion of the part of your mind you can control? Well, picture this. An intelligent, well-prepared teacher stands at the front of the class holding her organized lesson plans and ready to put her knowledge to work for her students. But her students are running around the room laughing and talking, staring out the window, or getting into fights. How much impact will the teacher have if she tries to start teaching before managing the chaos in her classroom? The beliefs, biases, and feelings in your unconscious mind are like the unruly students in the classroom. Until you can manage the chaos in your unconscious mind, your conscious mind cannot do its job.

An awareness of how your unconscious mind works can help you better understand why you do the things you do. This awareness can help you consciously change the things that create problems for you. With this knowledge, you can significantly improve your thinking and decision-making. You will also understand what drives other people so you can improve your relationships and positively influence others.

The unconscious mind is fast, effortless, and automatic. It is where our beliefs, feelings, and habits reside. It constantly monitors our environment and processes incoming information in real time. Since our evolutionary survival depended on identifying threats, our unconscious is always on the alert for potentially negative information. It makes snap judgments about what is happening now based on our past experiences, conditioning, and perspectives. Our unconscious minds are too busy to be fact checkers, so accuracy is not the highest priority.

In contrast, the conscious mind is slower and more contemplative. It is rational rather than emotional. It prizes accuracy over speed, so it thoughtfully responds to our environment rather than automatically reacting to it. It allows us to intentionally choose our own goals and then logically figure out how to achieve them. Whereas our unconscious minds are focused exclusively on the past and present, our conscious minds can also help us plan for a better future.

A common metaphor refers to the conscious mind as the rider and the unconscious mind as an elephant or horse. The implication is that the smaller rider attempts to direct the bigger animal to go where the rider wants it to go, but the animal has a mind of its own. The rider has a purpose, but the animal has the power.

Another metaphor is to think of the conscious mind as the parent and the unconscious mind as the child. A good parent provides their child with love and affection, but also with direction and protection. The child wants what they want, with no regard for consequences. The parent knows that not everything the child wants is good for them. Sometimes the parent must say no.

Whatever metaphor you use, you can see that problems arise when your conscious mind wants one thing, and your unconscious mind wants something else. They sometimes have conflicting goals. For instance, your conscious goal may be to improve your relationship with your boss in order to get a promotion, but if your unconscious goal is to boost your ego and prove you're smarter than your boss, you may sabotage your own efforts. When your conscious and unconscious are not in sync, you are literally of two minds.

If you consciously manage your unconscious mind, you will have more control over the direction of your life. If you don't, your unconscious mind will react to the people and events in your life the way it always has, and you'll get similar results to what you have in the past. You can influence your unconscious because you can talk to yourself whenever you want. When thoughts or feelings bubble up from your unconscious, you can consciously think about whether or not they're helpful. If they're in alignment with your chosen goals, great. If they're not, you can challenge and change them.

Be prepared to feel strange when you start to change how you think and behave. It won't feel natural. But much of what feels natural isn't. It's a product of your environment. If you are from the United States, it feels natural to drive on the right side of the road. If you are from the United Kingdom, it feels natural to drive on the left side of the road. Neither is natural, both are learned.

That uneasy feeling you experience when you first start doing something different is just your brain resisting change. Change takes energy, so no change for you means less drain on your brain.

Fortunately, researchers have discovered that our brains can change throughout our lives. The concept is known as neuroplasticity, which is the ability of the brain to reorganize itself by forming new neural connections. The new connections form in response to learning and new experiences, which you can actively pursue to upgrade your thinking skills. Neuroplasticity allows you to form new habits and discard old habits. You can rewire your brain by what you consciously focus on. The more you think, feel, or do something, the more natural it will become.

Your unconscious mind will adapt to change if you push past the initial resistance. The positive changes you implement will then become your new normal, requiring less energy going forward. Your unconscious mind can be changed, but it will never initiate change. That is the responsibility of your conscious mind, which is the focus of Parts Two and Three.

Since an estimated 95 percent of our cognitive activity is unconscious, let's explore unconscious beliefs, biases, and feelings. Understanding your unconscious mind will help you better understand yourself and other people. It will also give you insights into what Buddhism has called the basic problem of life: dissatisfaction. Things happen that you don't want, and things you want don't happen. You can overcome a great deal of dissatisfaction once you understand the flawed beliefs and negative emotions that cause it. This understanding will help you become more compassionate toward others, who are in the same unconscious boat as you.

Beliefs

Many of the beliefs you hold were not consciously formed. You did not conduct in-depth research and analysis and then choose your beliefs based on hard evidence. Most of your beliefs come from the opinions of other people, starting with the opinions of your family of origin. Your unconscious mind does not question. It simply accepts what it picks up from your environment, which includes input from your family, friends, and culture. Once absorbed, beliefs spread like viruses. You may not even know who you got them from, or when. You may know *what* you believe, but not *why* you believe it.

Regardless of how you originally picked up a belief, once your unconscious mind gets ahold of it, it won't easily let it go. If someone challenges your beliefs, you may get defensive. You might even be able to prove (to your satisfaction, not theirs) that you are right. One way to do this is through the confirmation bias. This bias entails looking for information that confirms what you already believe, which is especially easy to do today. You can find data that supports whatever personal, political, religious, business, social, economic, or other belief you hold. Of course, those who disagree with you can also find evidence to support their positions.

Another way you pick up beliefs is from your personal experiences. No one indoctrinated you with these beliefs; you unconsciously picked them up based on your interpretation of your firsthand experiences. These beliefs can be a valuable source of information, but they are also subject to error. For one thing, beliefs that were once true can become outdated. Some people and businesses continue to believe they know the best way to do something based on what worked in the past. But times change, and some past experiences are no longer relevant. Conscious thought and experimentation can help you evaluate whether a belief is still valid.

Another reason personal experience does not always produce reliable beliefs is that perceptions are sometimes inaccurate. If you experienced something when you were calm, clear-headed, observant, objective, and rational, your perception might be accurate. However, if you were emotional, tired, distracted, or biased for or against a person or situation, your perception may be flawed. Even if you think you are being objective, you are still filtering your experiences through your unique viewpoint. When you remember something later, you don't recall the exact words or events. What you recall is your interpretation of what was said and done based on your thoughts and feelings at the time. You have undoubtedly been in situations where your recollection of an incident was different from someone else's. Interestingly, we believe we know what really happened because we were there. Well, yes, but so were they. We tend to think that we know the truth, and anyone who disagrees with us is either lying or clearly doesn't remember what happened. Our beliefs are formed based on what we experienced, which may or may not reflect reality. Humbling, but true.

Determining whether a belief is true or false is not always easy to do. Further complicating matters is that your belief in something can make it true. For instance, if you believe you are not an interesting person, you may feel self-conscious in conversations. Because you feel self-conscious, you may be thinking about what others are thinking of you instead of paying attention to the conversation. Because you are focused on yourself and not what's being talked about, you are unlikely to add anything of interest. Hence, your thought that you are not interesting makes you less interesting. It becomes a self-fulfilling prophecy.

If your belief in a thing makes it seem true for you, why not consciously choose better beliefs? Beliefs are just working assumptions, after all. Rather than question if a belief is true or false, question whether it is helpful or harmful. Is it helpful to believe you're not interesting? No. So replace that belief with one that is more useful, like "I am interested in what others have to say." Or, "I connect better with people when I listen to what they say instead of thinking about what I'm going to say." Or, "I'm more relaxed when I'm fully engaged in a conversation and not trying to impress anyone." If the goal is to become more interesting, you can tackle it indirectly by consciously focusing on beliefs that make a person more interesting.

An alternative is using affirmations to directly counter the destructive belief, like telling yourself you are an interesting person when you really believe the opposite. The reason such affirmations often fail to work is that the unconscious mind doesn't believe them. If you tell yourself you're interesting while still unconsciously thinking you're boring, nothing changes. The missing element is action. By combining affirmations with a change in your behavior, you can change your unconscious mind. For instance, if you think you're boring, do something you find interesting. When you become interested in something, you become more interesting to others who are interested in the same thing.

Beliefs are not carved in stone. They are not sacred. Throughout history, widely held beliefs (erroneously called facts at the time) turned out to be false. The earth is not flat, the sun does not revolve around the earth, and rain dances do not bring rain. Beliefs help us navigate the world and filter incoming information so that we are not constantly overwhelmed. Beliefs are there to serve us, not the other way around. Beliefs *should* change throughout our lives as we become wiser. We would certainly not expect a 20-year old to hold the same beliefs they held as a 10-year old. So why would we expect a 60-year old to still believe what they did at 50? Our beliefs should evolve as we do. Our consciousness gives us the ability to upgrade our beliefs and our lives. As philosopher Henri Bergson noted, "To exist is to change, to change is to mature, to mature is to go on creating oneself endlessly."

Your beliefs drive your thoughts. Optimistic beliefs lead to positive thoughts. Pessimistic beliefs lead to negative thoughts. If something in your life isn't working as well as you'd like, question your beliefs about it. Uncovering the belief that is behind your dissatisfaction is the first step in changing it. You may think that your beliefs constitute who you are, but they don't. They simply reflect ideas about reality that you have accumulated over time. When you think about it, it's liberating to know that your beliefs can be changed – by you.

Biases

Now we're going to get a little more technical and talk about the cognitive biases that reside in our unconscious minds. Cognitive biases are faulty beliefs that cause us to automatically react rather than rationally respond. They distort the way we see the world. They impact our reasoning, judgments, and decision-making and can cause irrational behavior. Cognitive biases arise when the unconscious mind looks for mental shortcuts to explain what's going on. When people think of biases, they often think of stereotypes or prejudices, such as unfairly characterizing someone based solely on their race, gender, or religion. However, cognitive biases extend well beyond stereotypes to include all systematic patterns of thinking that are not based on logic. Cognitive biases are sometimes referred to as cognitive errors or heuristics.

Intelligence does not protect you from cognitive biases; in fact, it can make them worse. The smarter you are, the better you can rationalize your beliefs and articulate your arguments in favor of them. That's why really smart people sometimes say and do really stupid things.

There are hundreds of cognitive biases. Following are some of the more common ones. As you read through them, think about which ones are most applicable to you. HINT: If you don't think you're susceptible to any of the biases, read the *bias blind spot* definition.

- **Actor-observer bias:** Blaming another person's negative behavior on their personality rather than the situation but blaming your negative behavior on the situation rather than your personality.
- **Anchoring effect:** Overemphasizing the first piece of information you hear when forming a judgment or making a decision.
- **Availability heuristic:** Believing that information that quickly comes to mind is more common than it really is, like thinking shark attacks are more common than they are after watching news coverage of a shark attack.
- **Bandwagon effect:** Believing something because so many other people believe it, regardless of whether or not it's true.
- **Base-rate neglect:** Ignoring statistical evidence and instead believing individual stories and interesting anecdotes.
- **Bias blind spot:** Failing to recognize your own biases and believing you are less biased than other people.
- **Black-and-white thinking:** Viewing situations and people in all-or-nothing terms, as if they were 100% positive or 100% negative, with no middle ground.
- **Blaming:** Refusing to take personal responsibility and instead believing other people are the cause of your problems and negative feelings.

- **Confirmation bias:** Looking for information or evidence to support what you already believe.
- **Conservatism bias:** Continuing to believe prior information even when new evidence has emerged that contradicts the prior information.
- **Consistency bias:** Remembering your past attitudes and behaviors as being the same as your current ones even though they have actually changed over time.
- **Egocentric bias:** Recalling past experiences in a way that makes you look good.
- **Emotional reasoning:** Letting your interpretation of reality be driven by your emotions.
- **Empathy gap:** Failing to understand people who are in a different state of mind than you, like not understanding someone who is depressed when you are not depressed.
- **Framing:** Drawing conclusions based on how information is presented rather than on the content of the information itself.
- **Gambler's fallacy:** Believing that if some event has occurred more (or less) frequently than usual, the streak is "due" to be broken, even though the event itself (like a coin flip) is random so the past has no bearing on what happens next.
- **Halo effect:** Perceiving a person as positive in all areas based on their positive traits in one area. This bias is often

applied to famous people like politicians, athletes, and actors.

- **Herd instinct:** Adopting the opinions and behaviors of the majority to feel safer and avoid conflict. Sadly, tragic events like the Holocaust can occur as a result of this bias.
- **Hindsight bias:** Filtering memories of past events through present knowledge, so those events look more predictable now than they did at the time.
- **Illusion of asymmetric insight:** Believing you know other people better than they know you.
- **Illusion of control:** Believing you can control outcomes that you can't control.
- **Inter-group bias:** Viewing people in your own group more favorably than people in other groups, which gives rise to prejudice and discrimination.
- **Mind reading:** Assuming you know what people are thinking without any proof of their actual thoughts.
- **Negativity bias:** Emphasizing negative experiences rather than positive ones. Also known as the pessimism bias.
- **Normalcy bias:** Believing that something won't happen because it has never happened before.
- **Ostrich effect:** Ignoring negative information (by burying your head in the sand) so you don't have to think about unpleasant facts.

- **Outcome bias:** Judging a decision by how it turned out rather than looking at the quality of the decision at the time it was made. This bias fails to consider other factors that affect outcomes, like getting lucky or unlucky.

- **Overgeneralizing:** Drawing conclusions based on individual incidents and applying them in broader contexts where they may not be applicable.

- **Planning fallacy:** Underestimating how long it will take to complete a task.

- **Post-purchase rationalization:** Convincing yourself a purchase you made was worth the money to justify your spending after the fact.

- **Projection bias:** Assuming others think the same way you do.

- **Recency effect:** Putting more weight on recent events and information than on earlier ones.

- **Rosy retrospection:** Rating past events more positively than you rated them when they occurred.

- **Self-fulfilling prophecy:** Engaging in behaviors that bring about results that confirm your beliefs.

- **Self-serving bias:** Crediting success to your personal characteristics but blaming failures on outside forces.

- **Stereotyping:** Believing a person in a group has certain qualities even when you know nothing about the person.

- **Sunk-cost fallacy:** Sticking with a bad decision because you've already invested so much time, money, or effort into it.

You can use the above list to go on a bias hunt when you're making important decisions. Before you act, run through the list to see if any of the biases apply. For instance, if you are about to invest more money in a losing stock, remembering the sunk-cost fallacy may prevent you from making an irrational decision. By reminding yourself of common biases, you will make better decisions.

As you play *The Thinking Game*, look for clues to determine which biases and beliefs have the biggest impact on your thoughts and behavior. You can use that information going forward. When you make a decision or take an action that doesn't work out, reflect on whether any biases or beliefs played a part in the outcome. By making the unconscious conscious, you will make smarter decisions in the future.

In addition to improving self-awareness, you will also better understand other people by looking for clues to their biases and behavior. If you think like a detective instead of a judge, you will begin to figure out what makes people think and behave the way they do. Knowing how people unconsciously think can improve your social skills. It allows you to anticipate what people will say or do before they say or do it. It helps you get along with others and get ahead at work. It strengthens your relationships with friends, family members, teammates, and coworkers. You'll also perform better against competitors because you'll be able to predict their moves before they make them.

If you think there was a *negativity bias* in the sections on beliefs, you're right. That was intentional. Your unconscious mind also holds many positive and accurate beliefs. But those beliefs are already working in your favor, so they don't require any additional action on your part. When you prune back your flawed beliefs and biases, you give your healthy beliefs more room to flourish.

Feelings

Feelings and emotions arise from the unconscious mind. Sometimes our emotions are triggered by external events, like having an emotional response to narrowly avoiding a car accident. Other times, our feelings are based on what we are thinking. For instance, thinking your boss is annoyed with you can cause you to feel anxiety even if your assumption is wrong. You can change your feelings by changing the thoughts that create them. You can also manage how you respond to what you're feeling.

Positive emotions such as joy, gratitude, love, inspiration, and serenity feel good and are good for you. These feelings improve your well-being, relationships, creativity, and problem-solving abilities. The more you focus on positive feelings, the more they become part of your normal attitude. Encouraging these feelings is not a Pollyanna approach to life that denies that bad things happen. It is a realistic philosophy that recognizes that your feelings and thoughts are related. Even when problems arise, you can optimistically seek a solution instead of pessimistically assuming you won't find one. You cannot simultaneously feel positive and negative emotions, so why not choose positive feelings? You can consciously cultivate these feelings by putting more emphasis on what is positive about a person or situation, rather than focusing on the negative aspects. Doing so will make you more positive, productive, and popular.

Negative emotions such as fear, worry, envy, anger, jealousy, and anxiety feel bad and are bad for you. They harm your health, relationships, and peace of mind. They make it hard to achieve a satisfying life. The most unhappy and insecure people are those who allow negative feelings to take up permanent residence in their unconscious minds. They dwell on thoughts that reinforce their negative feelings. They believe other people and situations are to blame for their misery and lack the awareness to know they bring it on themselves. As a result, they often feel lonely and misunderstood. You can instead adopt the mindset of the ancient Stoics who believed that tranquility comes from consciously dropping negative emotions.

The Thinking Game

One of the ways you can manage how you feel is to challenge what you're thinking. When negative feelings arise, question them. You will often find that the problem isn't the situation; it's your interpretation of the situation. It's not what happened; it's the meaning you read into what happened. For instance, we create a lot of anxiety for ourselves by taking things personally. We think that things are being done to us, instead of realizing they are just being done. Don't believe everything you think.

Fear is the strongest of the negative feelings, and it often shows up as worry, doubt, guilt, or anger. Think about each of these emotions. Worry is the fear of something going wrong. Doubt is the fear of being wrong. Guilt is the fear of having done something wrong. Anger is the fear of being wronged by someone. These emotions are all just different forms of mental suffering caused by the feeling that something isn't right. We think things should be a certain way and it feels wrong if they're not. These types of fear are all in our heads; they are not objective conditions in the outside world. Don't believe everything you feel.

You physically feel negative emotions in your body, but they are caused by what's going on in your mind. Think of how quickly negative feelings evaporate when you change your thinking. For instance, if you thought your family forgot your birthday, your anxiety turns to joy when you realize they planned a surprise party for you. The anxiety was manufactured by your unconscious mind which leaped to a negative conclusion about what was going on.

What you were thinking was never true. What you were feeling was never justified despite how real it felt to you.

Instead of assuming negative feelings are justified, try challenging them *while they're happening*. The problem isn't the feeling; it's what you do with it. Do you allow it to linger? Do you instantly try to get rid of it by doing something rash? Or do you question it? Next time you catch yourself feeling worried, guilty, angry, or upset, ask yourself why you are feeling that way. Is it based on facts? Or just on your interpretation of what *might* be going on? Is it possible you're mistaken? Is the feeling helping you in any way? Is it accomplishing anything positive? If it's not, shift your thoughts in a more productive direction and your feelings will follow.

For example, if you are feeling guilty, ask yourself why. Did you do something wrong? Or are you just afraid someone else will think you did something wrong? Like not calling your mother back right away or not accepting a friend's invitation. A great quote attributed to Confucius is, "If you look into your heart and you find nothing wrong there, what is there to worry about? What is there to fear?" Good advice. If you decide to stop feeling guilty when you honestly believe you've done nothing wrong, you'll become immune to guilt trips – real or imagined.

Negative feelings can become habitual and harden into attitudes, so don't let them hang around and become familiar. Label them and question them. If you catch yourself worrying, say "worrying" to yourself and then refocus on something more productive. If the feeling of worry persists, question it. "Hey, Worry, what's up?" Then listen to hear if it has anything new to report, or if it's just rehashing the same old things. Blah, blah, blah. You take away the power of the negative emotion if you challenge it.

If you examine negative feelings, you will begin to see the truth about your thinking. Forget why someone said or did something, and instead ask yourself why it bothers you. Why are you reacting the way you are? Do you think they're right? If you do, is there anything you want to change as a result? If so, work on it. If not, don't worry about it. They're entitled to their opinion, but that doesn't mean you have to share it. You don't have to take things personally, even if someone meant them to be taken personally.

Feelings can be a great indicator of what is, and is not, working in your life. Use your feelings to gauge where changes are needed. Try to stand back and view them from a detached perspective. If someone else were in the same situation experiencing the same feelings, what would you tell them? Being objective will make it easier to manage your feelings and make the right decision on what, if anything, to do about them. You'll be able to ask yourself questions like: Why am I *really* feeling this way? Am I being overly sensitive? Am I just reacting out of jealousy? Am I just tired and irritable today? Or is there a real issue here?

Think of negative feelings like indicator lights on the dashboard of your car. These warning lights indicate a *potentially* dangerous condition that needs to be checked. Sometimes, the warning lights are a false alarm, like when the "check engine light" comes on because you didn't screw your gas cap on tight enough. Negative feelings can also be false alarms. When a negative feeling arises, question whether there's a real issue. If there is, address it. If there's not, shift your attention elsewhere. You know, some people call those dashboard lights *idiot lights*. Some negative feelings are idiotic.

Acknowledge your feelings, but realize you have a choice as to how you respond to them. If the issue is all in your head, you can shake it off and regain your peace of mind. You can calm yourself down. Remaining emotional won't solve the problem because you can't think clearly when you're emotional. If after consciously thinking about how you feel you still believe there is a real issue, you can rationally think about how best to address it.

You can also consciously cultivate the positive feelings you would like to have, rather than leaving them to chance. For instance, if you want to be more confident, tell yourself that you already are and think back to instances where you have felt confident. You might as well use the confirmation bias in your favor. If you struggle to change your thoughts or feelings, try changing your behavior first. For instance, if it bothers you when someone else is the center of attention, don't try to force yourself to stop feeling that way. Instead, let them have the attention. In fact, be the one to give it to them. Compliment them or ask them questions about themselves. Put yourself in control of your feelings by acting as if it doesn't bother you when someone else has the limelight. Why should it bother you? You're confident. You are not so insecure that you need the attention.

The more you intentionally seek a more positive state of mind, the more often you'll experience it. Seek, and you will find. Pick a feeling you want to have more of and then behave in a way that corresponds to what you want to feel. If you generally focus on the negative, intentionally seek the positive. If you normally criticize and complain, consciously express praise and gratitude. Have fun with it. Make it a game. When you change how you think, you'll change how you feel. As philosophical writer James Allen wrote, "A man will find as he alters his thoughts towards things and other people, things and other people will alter towards him." Test it for yourself. It's interesting to see how people react when you act differently toward them. If nothing else, you'll confuse them.

We all experience a wide range of emotions, but you don't have to be controlled by them. It's your game; be a player, not a piece. If something isn't working out, don't stew about it. If you can change the situation, change it. If you can't change the situation, change your feelings about it and move on to something you can control.

Managing your emotions is your responsibility. When someone pushes your buttons, it's easy to think they are the problem. But they're just doing what they do. You're not upset because of what they do; you're upset because of how you think it affects you. For instance, you might feel irritated when a family member is irresponsible because then you *have to* clean up their mess. Really? Says who? Maybe if you quit fixing things, they'd quit breaking them. And if they don't, allow them the opportunity to experience the consequences of their actions.

Don't blame other people for how you feel. If something they say or do upsets you, ask yourself why. Do you want their approval and fear you aren't getting it? Are you afraid of confrontation and think they're trying to provoke you? Do you feel insecure and think they're making you look bad to others? Be a detective and figure out why you feel the way you do. Focus on your part, not theirs. Remember, they're playing their game, and you need to play yours.

Your unconscious mind wants to maintain the status quo. It wants what is familiar, regardless of whether it's good or bad. If you have chronic issues with certain people or situations, you will feel uncomfortable when you first break from your normal pattern of reacting to them. But nothing will change if you continue to react the same way every time. You choose to let things bother you, and you can choose not to. You have that power.

When you understand why you feel the way you do, you'll be able to change how you feel and what you do. Initially, the same circumstances may trigger the same feelings, but now you'll know what's happening. "Oh yeah, this is me feeling guilty because Mom is unhappy, and I feel responsible for making her happy." Then instead of your normal reaction when she complains about being unhappy, you could say something like, "I'm sorry you're unhappy. I love you and wish things were different for you. Here's what I can do. What do you think you could do to improve things?" And remember you cannot make another person happy, no matter how much you care about them. We are all susceptible to the thoughts, moods, and feelings of others, so limit the time you spend with chronically unhappy people. As seventeenth-century philosopher Baltasar Gracian admonished, "Do not die of another's misery."

Do what you think is the right thing to do, not just what is expected of you. It will take courage, and there may be some blowback. If you have always reacted a certain way, some people may not take kindly to you changing. Others may say, "It's about time." Control your own moves and let others control theirs. Don't be a pawn, and don't try to make anyone else one.

If you're not satisfied with some aspect of your life, it may be because your unconscious beliefs and feelings conflict with what you consciously desire. Until you bring those unconscious saboteurs into the light, they will continue to hinder your efforts to change. If you want to change, you must decide to be driven by new beliefs of your own choosing. It takes more energy initially to consciously commit to new beliefs and act on them, but if you persist, your unconscious mind will accept them. Once your unconscious mind embraces your new beliefs, it will automatically use them to shape your future thoughts, feelings, and actions – requiring considerably less conscious effort on your part.

The unconscious mind is bound by nature and nurture. It is instinctive and effortless. It is also powerful and can help you achieve your goals if it is properly managed. Your conscious mind is management; if it is a good leader, your unconscious mind will be a good follower.

In Part Two, we'll explore how to master conscious thinking, which is where your freedom lies. You'll pick up strategies for improving your mindset, strengthening your thinking skills, and using effective thinking techniques. You'll also be provided with specific questions to trigger better thinking in all major areas of your life.

Part Two:

How to Improve Conscious Thinking

Chapter 3:

Developing a Thinking Mindset

"As human beings, our greatness lies not so much in being able to remake the world…as in being able to remake ourselves."

—attributed to Mahatma Gandhi

The thinking mindset is a mental attitude that seeks to understand the world and how to effectively live in it. People with a thinking mindset have developed certain traits that make it easier for them to figure out what they need to know and do to make the most of their life. They actively look for information, knowledge, and wisdom to help them make good decisions that align with their goals. They are like a detective, researcher, and philosopher rolled into one.

If some of the traits that comprise the thinking mindset do not come naturally to you, developing them may take a little time and practice. It is time well spent. Not only do the traits make life more enjoyable, but they also significantly improve your success rate. A thinking mindset gives you freedom. Freedom to choose how you will live. Freedom to decide what you will do. Freedom from the dissatisfaction that plagues so many people because they don't know what they want or how to get it.

When you develop a thinking mindset, your attitude toward life changes. Life becomes much more interesting. You become fully engaged in the game. You have no interest in going through the motions. You actively seek greater challenges and goals. You want to learn, grow, contribute, and get the most out of life. You don't just want to keep your head down and coast until the game is over. You want to play.

High achievers like Leonardo da Vinci, Marcus Aurelius, Marie Curie, Stephen Hawking, and Benjamin Franklin had a thinking mindset. By studying how people, nature, and things worked, they were able to succeed at doing what interested them most in life: creating art, ruling empires, pioneering scientific research, exploring the universe, and inventing products and services that improved the lives of millions of people. You can achieve your own definition of success by cultivating the following thinking traits.

Curiosity

Curiosity is a strong desire to know or learn something.

Curious people love learning. They have a strong desire to know how things work and why things are the way they are. Their favorite question is...Why? Albert Einstein said, "I have no special talents. I am only passionately curious." Curious people learn faster and remember more of what they learn. Their interest in figuring things out causes them to ask lots of questions. It also causes them to experiment in order to increase their understanding of what works and what doesn't. Their curiosity stimulates their minds, so they are able to generate and execute great ideas. In the process of satisfying their curiosity, they become more knowledgeable and successful. They build expertise. They are interesting people to know.

Contrast that with people lacking in curiosity. Their conversations, actions, and life tend to be dull and repetitive. They don't ask questions, because they don't care about the answers or think they already know them. They don't read thought-provoking books, because they'd rather be entertained than informed. As a result, they rarely learn anything new. They think of learning as something they were forced to do in school. They view learning as rote memorization of useless information rather than seeing it as a chance to improve their lives and the lives of others. Year after year, they think, say, and do the same things. They are bored and boring.

If you're curious to see how you can strengthen this trait, the following are some challenges to get you started.

Curiosity Challenges:

Challenge #1: Learn about something that interests you. Pick a topic you would be curious to know more about and go learn things. Read about it, discuss it with others, and figure out what it's all about. If it's a skill you want to learn, study how it works, observe others doing it, and try doing it yourself. You can choose something personal, like learning to cook something, make something, or understand something. Or you can pick something work-related, like learning how some new technology works or figuring out how a competitor operates. Leonardo da Vinci kept notebooks full of different things that piqued his curiosity. He wrote about (and drew sketches of) his many interests and experiments. You may not be interested in flying machines or underpainting techniques, but you can use Leonardo's idea and create your own notebooks on topics, skills, and issues that interest you.

Challenge #2: Get in the habit of asking questions. Think like a journalist and ask who, what, when, where, why, and how questions to increase your knowledge base. No one knows everything, but many people avoid asking questions for fear of looking stupid. Not asking questions is a sure way to remain ignorant. Successful people ask questions all the time, and it shortens their learning curve. Sam Walton drove retailers crazy with all his questions about how they did business, but it helped him turn Walmart into one of the world's most successful businesses. In addition to increasing your expertise, asking questions gives you greater insight into how other people think and flatters them that you're interested in what they have to say. Win. Win. Win.

Challenge #3: Put yourself in an unfamiliar situation. When everything is familiar and comfortable, there's nothing new to stimulate your mind and trigger your curiosity. Broaden your perspectives by exposing yourself to new people, places, activities, and things. Instead of talking to the same people all the time, seek the opinions of people whose backgrounds, occupations, political party, socioeconomic status, gender, or culture, are different from yours. Instead of going to the same old places, try new and materially different types of restaurants, shops, entertainment venues, and travel destinations. Instead of using the same products, mix it up. If you're usually high-tech, do something low-tech to accomplish the same thing. If you're usually low-tech, go high-tech. Instead of doing the same activities, try something different that requires your active participation and is outside your normal skill set. For instance, if you're the analytical type, take an art class. If you're the creative type, take an accounting course. When you push yourself to do something that makes you uncomfortable, you rekindle your curiosity and learn things you can apply in other settings. Side benefits: it increases your confidence and makes you more interesting.

Observation

Observation is closely watching someone or something to gain information.

Observant people pay attention to what's going on *within* them and *around* them. They are self-aware. They notice their own thoughts and actions and reflect on why they do what they do. This helps them see the truth about themselves and allows them to make positive changes. It also helps them see the humor in life as they observe how silly and petty we can be. For instance, when Stoic philosopher Seneca observed his own petty reaction to not being seated in a manner befitting his status, he told himself, "You lunatic. What difference does it make what part of the couch you put your weight on?" Observant people also pay attention to what's happening around them. Because of social niceties, political correctness, or ulterior motives, people do not always say what they're thinking. So observant people pay close attention to nonverbal cues, which gives them valuable information and helps them communicate better. They observe expressions, body language, and tone of voice to pick up cues to what people are really thinking. Observant people notice details that others miss. Their heightened awareness allows them to quickly spot patterns, anomalies, features, issues, and changes. Because they are among the first to notice details and data, they spot new trends and identify problems before anyone else. This allows them to take advantage of opportunities and avoid risks before others even know they exist.

In contrast, oblivious people lack self-awareness and have no clue about what is going on around them. They are lost in their own world. You probably know people who can't seem to take a hint. Even if you are tapping your foot, glancing at the door, and emphasizing how much work you have to do, the other person just keeps on talking. They are so focused on what they think and want that they don't notice anything or anyone else. They are blind to the signals from other people and their environment. They don't see what is obvious to everyone else. Their lack of awareness damages their relationships and limits their chances for personal and professional success.

If your powers of observation aren't what you would like them to be, pay attention to the following challenges.

Observation Challenges:

Challenge #1: Mentally prepare to be observant. Before an important event or activity, take a few minutes to get in the right frame of mind. First, clear your mind of anything that's not related to what you're getting ready to do. If your mind is on other things, you won't be fully present or aware. You can always jot down notes to remind you of other issues to address later but stop thinking about them now. Second, think about your purpose or goal for the upcoming activity. What do you want to accomplish? By thinking about your specific goal beforehand, you prime your mind to focus on the goal later when you're in the middle of the activity. Finally, remind yourself to be observant during the event or activity, so you don't miss things because you're lost in your thoughts instead of paying attention to what's going on around you. Now, you're good to go.

Challenge #2: Practice situational awareness when you're alone. Your intentions to be more observant may be forgotten the minute you start interacting with other people. One way to become more aware is to practice being observant when you're by yourself. For instance, think about your normal behavior when doing solo activities like driving, exercising, running errands, or waiting in a doctor's office. Are you usually lost in thought, talking or texting on your phone, reading a magazine, or listening to music? If so, set aside the mental and physical distractions and use that time to look around you. What are other people doing, saying, reading, or wearing? Are they hurrying or taking their time? Do they seem happy, sad, bored, angry, or preoccupied? Notice your surroundings, too. Are they nice or run down? Crowded or deserted? Well-lit or dark? Becoming more observant will not only make you more successful, but it will also keep you safer. According to safety experts, many victims of accidents and crime could have avoided their fate if they had been paying more attention to what was happening around them.

Challenge #3: Ask yourself questions to become more self-aware. One of the primary reasons people don't get what they want in life is because they don't know what they want. By asking yourself questions, you can figure out what matters most to you and how you are helping or hurting yourself in your efforts to get it or keep it. Take some time to observe your thoughts and actions. Ask yourself questions like, Why am I feeling this way? For instance, if you find yourself in a good mood after spending time with a friend, ask what it is about them that makes you feel good? Are there qualities they have that you would like to emulate? Conversely, if you are upset because someone you don't even particularly like or respect slighted you, you might want to ask yourself why you care so much about what other people think of you. If you are upset about something, ask yourself why. What happened that you didn't want? What did you want that didn't happen? Why does that matter to you? Follow the ancient Greek aphorism to "Know thyself," and you'll be able to clarify what you want, why you want it, and why it matters.

Persistence

Persistence is continuing a course of action despite facing difficulties.

The Thinking Game

Persistent people know that the only way to achieve a goal is to relentlessly pursue it. When they want to know or do something, they do not give up until they've achieved their goal. They continue to turn things over in their mind. They ask for input from others and gather information. If they run into problems, they find a way around them. They may sometimes put a problem or issue aside temporarily, but they will come back to it until they figure it out. They are tenacious. Their desire to achieve their objective causes them to continually ask questions until they arrive at answers that satisfy them. If they try one thing and that doesn't work, they try something else. Eventually, they find a way to succeed.

Contrast that with quitters. They may start out enthusiastically, but they give up as soon as they encounter challenges. They want things to be easy, so they bail when things turn out to be harder than expected. They are master rationalizers. They can provide twenty-one excuses for why something didn't work out, and it is never through any fault of theirs. They are more concerned with their image than their results, so the blaming bias kicks in causing them to attribute their failures to other people or circumstances. The truth is that they lack the discipline to follow through. They may even say they changed their mind and no longer want what they said they wanted (a.k.a. the sour grapes excuse). Regardless of how they justify their failure to persist, the end result is that they do not achieve their most important goals in life.

If you want to be more persistent, be sure to complete the following challenges.

Persistence Challenges:

Challenge #1: Persist at something you know how to do but aren't doing. To persist at a goal that you aren't sure how to achieve requires a higher level of persistence. Examples might include addressing a chronic health problem or figuring out an ideal retirement plan. To build up your persistence muscle, start with something you already know how to do but aren't consistently doing. For instance, if you have a habit of hitting the snooze button in the morning, discipline yourself to get up as soon as the alarm goes off for the next 10 days. Or choose another habit you want to change for which you know what to do but aren't doing it, like working out on a regular schedule. If you miss a day, don't get discouraged and give up. Try again. Practice persistence on simpler things and then work up to the more challenging things that you aren't yet sure how to do.

Challenge #2: Track your persistence. There is something psychologically motivating in being able to visually see your progress. To become more persistent, track your efforts. For instance, comedian Jerry Seinfeld had a goal to work on his jokes every day. On days he wrote new material, he would put a big red

X on his calendar, and his goal was to never break the chain. This works well for tracking your persistence in establishing new habits, like meditating every day. It also works well for tracking your persistence in stopping bad habits, like drinking alcohol in excess. Persistence can also be tracked for achievement goals. For instance, if you are writing a book, you can track your persistence by noting how many words you wrote each day or how many hours you spent writing each day.

Challenge #3: Envision the future results of your persistence.
There was a reason you set out to do something in the first place. What was that reason? When trying to figure something out becomes too difficult, or you just don't feel like doing it, it's easy to quit. So most people do. But success comes from persistence. If you're tempted to quit, take a few minutes to remind yourself why you're doing this. What results are you seeking? How would it feel to achieve them? Take your mind off your obstacles and rekindle your desire for the outcome. Quitting may feel good now, but what will you wish you had done a week, month, or year from now? When Current You resists, make sure Future You persists.

Calmness

Calmness is being free from agitation or strong emotions.

Calm people maintain emotional self-control, which allows them to think clearly. When negative feelings surface, they consciously shut them down before they can hijack their thinking. They are cool under pressure. While others may become anxious in difficult situations, they remain focused on the task at hand. They aren't thinking about themselves or what others are thinking about them; they're thinking about the best way to handle the current issue or problem. They don't get upset over minor irritations. Nor do they worry about things that could go wrong or things they can't control. They focus on the things they can control, which are their thoughts, feelings, and actions. They make good leaders and friends because they get things done and are a calming presence for those around them. Calmness is power.

Contrast calm, cool, and collected thinkers with people who are overly emotional. They can be up one minute and down the next. They are easily knocked off kilter when things don't go their way. You probably know people who are frequently agitated or excitable. They may refer to themselves as passionate, but others find them to be exhausting. People often feel they must tiptoe around them for fear of setting off an emotional storm. They are quick to take offense and take everything personally. They may display anger, fear, paranoia, despair, or other negative emotions out of proportion to the situation that triggered their emotional outburst. When they are emotional, they are unable to think clearly. As a result, they tend to make irrational decisions, or they become indecisive and cannot make a decision at all. They are difficult to be around and often end up lonely and unhappy.

Because they cannot tolerate even minor irritations, they become overwhelmed when major ones occur. A lack of composure is a weakness that leads to a dissatisfying life.

If you would like to be calmer, take a deep breath and then take on the following challenges.

Calmness Challenges:

Challenge #1: Pause before responding when issues arise. When something upsetting happens, your unconscious mind reacts automatically before your conscious mind has a chance to respond thoughtfully. If you give in to the negative feelings that emerge, they will cause you to break down or blow up. When minor irritations occur, shrug them off. Annoying as they are, is it worth disturbing your peace of mind and lashing out at others because your computer isn't working, your waiter got your order wrong, or someone blocked the grocery aisle with their shopping cart? Take a deep breath and shake it off. For more significant problems or provocations, try not to respond right away, or you may make the situation worse. Take a moment to calm down and center yourself. In that time, you may realize that you overreacted to the situation or possibly even completely misread it. By waiting to respond, you will be able to think more clearly about what you want to do to address the situation. You'll make more rational decisions. You'll also earn the respect of reasonable people and won't incur the wrath of unreasonable and vindictive people. Pick your battles or someone else may sink your battleship.

Challenge #2: Maintain a regular calming practice. It's much easier to remain calm in the first place than to calm yourself down once you become emotional. Having a regular practice like meditation can help you become a calmer person. Then, when stressful situations occur, you will be better prepared to handle them calmly. We are all wired differently, so find what is calming for you. If meditation doesn't work for you, maybe going for a walk, listening to music, practicing yoga, writing in a journal, or something else will. Oddly enough, even walking through a cemetery can be calming, because it reminds you to put things into perspective. You're alive, and most of the things that upset you won't matter in the long run. Whatever calming practice you choose, do it regularly so you will have a peaceful, easy feeling that won't let you down.

Challenge #3: Seek a calming influence outside yourself. Everyone should have someone or something they can turn to when they are troubled. It may be a loving and supportive spouse. For instance, my husband can calm me down with a hug or by using humor when appropriate to "calm my ass down." Other family members or friends can also be calming influences. As can a pet who is always happy to see you; a professional coach, counselor, or therapist; or a spiritual, religious, or philosophical source, such as Buddhism, Christianity, or Stoicism. When you are unable to calm yourself down, it is helpful to know you are not alone. If you regularly spend time with calming influences, you will become a calmer person yourself.

Honesty

Honesty is being truthful with yourself and others.

No one is completely honest 100 percent of the time, but honest people are more truthful than most. They are realists. They understand that they cannot deal with a situation if they deny that it exists. Even though they sometimes fall short of their goal, their intent is to be honest with themselves and others. They are interested in the truth, which makes them open-minded. They understand that no one has a monopoly on the truth, not even them. As a result, they are not emotionally invested in being right. They know they don't have all the answers. If someone else has a better answer, they are happy to accept it. They seek solutions, not credit. They do not do things along party lines. If they believe the person, group, company, or political party they support is wrong on an issue, they are not afraid to say so. They are intellectually honest. They follow the advice from the Master in *The Analects* of Confucius: "A gentleman does not approve of a person because he expresses a certain opinion, nor does he reject an opinion because it is expressed by a certain person."

Their honesty is refreshing to others and earns them trust. Being honest also raises their self-respect and self-esteem. Because they know who they are and what they stand for, they are more authentic than the vast majority of people who worry about appearances and fitting in.

At the opposite extreme are people who have allowed dishonesty to become part of their character. It is not a place they occasionally visit; it's where they live. They deceive themselves, as well as others. If they are uncomfortable with certain truths about themselves, they deny them and try to project the opposite. They rationalize away anything that doesn't support their desired self-image. Because they don't acknowledge their shortcomings, they are powerless to change them. They delude themselves for so long that they come to believe their own lies. They also lie to other people when it suits their purposes. Sometimes their deceit is because they are trying to get something from someone. Other times it is because they want to portray a more flattering image of themselves. If the image they create of themselves is too far from the truth, they may eventually suffer a mental breakdown. Our minds are predisposed to protect our egos, but they can only stretch so far away from reality before they snap. Honesty trumps delusion.

If you honestly want to work on this trait, consider these challenges.

Honesty Challenges:

Challenge #1: Objectively assess your strengths and weaknesses. Honesty starts with being honest with yourself. As Shakespeare said in *Hamlet*: "This above all: to thine own self be true, and it must follow, as the night the day, thou canst not then be false to any man." Think about what you like and dislike about yourself. No one is perfect, and the point of the challenge is to give you a balanced view of yourself. Thinking about your strengths boosts your confidence. Thinking about your weaknesses keeps you humble. Your weaknesses list may consist of two types of items: those you cannot change and those you can. If you dislike your height, that's not a weakness, it's a feature. Accept it and move on. For the weaknesses you can change, decide which ones you care enough about to want to improve and create a plan of action to do it.

Challenge #2: Don't compare yourself to other people. One of the main reasons people are dishonest is because they want to look good to others, or at least not look bad. When you try to impress others, it's tempting to embellish your accomplishments and how great your life is. Ironically, when we brag about ourselves, people tend to think less favorably of us. When you're dishonest with others, it is disturbing to your mind. You feel like a phony. Worse, if you do it often enough and for an extended period, you begin to blur the line until you can't see the truth anymore. At that point, people stop believing anything you say. The solution to image-based dishonesty is to stop comparing yourself to other people. Just be you and let them be them.

Challenge #3: Pay attention to criticism and learn from it. The Stoic Seneca observed that the worse a man is, the less likely he is to accept constructive criticism. You've probably observed this yourself when someone is defensive over even the smallest of things. Our image of ourselves is shaped by our thoughts, but other people form an image of us based on our behavior. Assuming no animosity, their observations of us are more objective than ours. If someone you love or respect offers you constructive criticism, assess whether what they're saying is true. If you've been told the same thing by multiple people, listen even more closely. You can even learn something from those who have ulterior motives for criticizing you, like those who are jealous, chronically unhappy, or who stand to gain by their criticism of you. Much of what they say may be garbage but consider whether there is any truth to what they're saying, since they may tell you things that others will not. Even in the case of social media trolls, there may occasionally be a helpful nugget in their harsh criticism of you or your work. If you're not aware of shortcomings that could be hindering your success and happiness, you can't change them. Honesty is the most effective policy.

Confidence

Confidence is trusting in your abilities, judgments, and personal qualities.

Confident people don't believe they know everything, but they trust that they will be able to find out what they need to know. They're optimistic. If they hear or read something that doesn't make sense to them, they ask questions and look for explanations. Insecure people worry about looking stupid; confident people don't. They know that asking questions helps them become better informed. Their questioning also enables them to figure out when someone else has made a mistake or is lying. Because they trust their own judgment, they rarely fall for cons and marketing ploys and are unlikely to be manipulated into doing something foolish. Their confidence increases their chances of success because they are courageous enough to try new things. While many people shy away from doing anything they might not be good at, self-assured people enjoy the challenge. Their life is richer because they go after what they really want in life instead of worrying about failure. They know failure is not fatal. They don't care what other people think of them, and paradoxically that makes people like them more. They're confident in who they are and don't feel the need to impress anyone. If you like them, great. If you don't, fine. They like themselves.

Contrast confident people with those lacking in confidence. Because they doubt their ability to do challenging things, they don't even try to do them. Their lack of confidence becomes a self-fulfilling prophecy. They doubt their ability to succeed, and their unconscious mind reinforces that belief. They're afraid to do anything they don't already know how to do, so they don't learn and grow. As a result, they don't live up to their potential. They play it safe in their personal and professional lives. Their lack of confidence is all in their head, but it's real to them. If they ever tiptoe outside their comfort zone, they quickly run back to it if things don't go perfectly – which, of course, they never do. They think they would pursue more challenging goals if they were more confident, but it is the pursuit of challenging goals that would make them more confident. Funny how that works.

If you're insecure about your confidence level, try the following challenges.

Confidence Challenges:

Challenge #1: Establish a baseline of confidence. Building your confidence is like building your credit or your résumé. Lenders want you to already have established credit before they will lend you money. Employers want you to already have work experience before they will hire you. But you have to start somewhere, so you usually get a small line of credit and an entry-level job to get started. Then you move up from there. Confidence works the same way; you build it a little at a time. Start with things that require a little confidence and grow from there. For instance, if you want to be more confident in social situations, attend an event where you don't know anyone, like a gallery opening or a business seminar. Set a goal to go up to at least three people during the event and strike up a conversation. The worse thing that's going to happen is you'll be rebuffed. Great, then go up to a fourth person. Make it a game to figure out what people respond well to versus what doesn't seem to work, and then adjust your strategy accordingly. The more you do it, the more confident you'll become in your social skills. You gain confidence by doing things you want to do but are afraid to do. Confidence begets confidence, just as success begets success.

Challenge #2: Validate yourself through positive self-talk. No one else can give you confidence, nor can they take it away. You don't need to be validated by anyone else. If you rely on others to make you feel good with their praise, you're also giving them the power to make you feel bad with their criticism or indifference. Self-validate with positive self-talk. Your fears will try to prevent you from doing anything risky, even if the risk is all in your head. Playing it safe makes for a boring life, so talk back to your fears. They're just bullies trying to get you to back down. Tell yourself you will be able to figure out what you need to know and do.

Instead of looking at uncertainty as a bad thing, see it as an opportunity to grow. Make it a game to think up different ways to overcome your challenges. If one thing doesn't work, try another. If you're nervous about trying something new, ask yourself what's the worst that can happen? Then figure out how to minimize the risk, assuming there is a risk worth minimizing. "I could be embarrassed" doesn't count. Once you've given yourself a pep talk and mustered some courage, immediately take action before your mind can change itself.

I've even seen positive self-talk work with a 3-year old. When my youngest nephew was little, we went bowling and he used a bowling ramp. After a couple of frames, I heard him whispering to himself. "I can do this. I can bowl like the big kids. I'm Superman. I can do anything." I leaned down and asked if he wanted to try to bowl without the ramp, and he said yes. His bowling ball took a long time to make it down the lane, but he did it and even knocked down a few pins. The moral of the story is to use positive self-talk...and lose the bowling ramp.

Challenge #3: Take the focus off yourself. Self-consciousness creates a lack of confidence. If you weren't so worried about looking bad or failing, you would just give things a go and see what happens. As long as you are preoccupied with your performance, you are likely to feel nervous, anxious, or stressed when you are in challenging or unfamiliar situations. You can take the pressure off yourself by focusing on your goal instead of yourself. For instance, if you have to give a speech, stop thinking about whether you'll do a good job or whether people will like you. Focus on the speech itself. What is the purpose of the speech? What are the main points you want to make? Who is the audience? How can you help them? Similarly, if you're feeling insecure in a social setting, focus on the people around you. Instead of thinking about what you should say, ask about them. Most people love talking about themselves, and it takes the pressure off you. A lack of confidence comes from comparing yourself to others; so don't. No need to worry about what people are thinking of you, because most of the time, they're not. They're thinking of themselves. It's only your preoccupation with yourself that is making you feel insecure. You cannot become more confident at something by avoiding it. By focusing on other people, the problem, the situation, the activity, or the goal instead of yourself, you'll feel more at ease and will begin to build real confidence.

By becoming more curious, observant, persistent, calm, honest, and confident, you'll develop a thinking mindset. These traits will make playing *The Thinking Game* easier, more enjoyable, and more rewarding. In addition to making you a more effective thinker, they'll also make your life more pleasant and fulfilling.

With the thinking mindset, you give yourself a big advantage in life. Think of it as your conditioning. If an athlete isn't mentally prepared for the game, no amount of skill, athleticism, or knowledge of the game is enough. They must have their head in the game. If their lack of confidence makes them tentative...or they aren't observing what's happening in the game...or they get angry over a foul and can't calm themselves down...or they quit trying when their team gets behind – they are not going to be winners. It's the same for you when you're playing *The Thinking Game*. Keep your head in the game. When you develop the thinking mindset and combine it with the skills and techniques covered in the next few chapters, you'll become unstoppable.

Chapter 4:

Strengthening Your Thinking Skills

"Man's greatness lies in his power of thought."

—attributed to Blaise Pascal

A thinking skill is an ability to use your mind intelligently. Despite the importance of thinking skills, they are rarely taught in schools or in the workplace. Instead, students are taught subjects, and employees are taught tasks. In other words, students and employees are taught what to think, but not how to think.

While many skills can help to improve thinking, four stand out: research, organization, analysis, and decision-making.

- Research is seeking and finding information
- Organization is putting information in order
- Analysis is making sense of information
- Decision-making is choosing what to do with information

These skills help you think more clearly, accurately, and efficiently. Sharpening these skills will allow you to get more done, in less time, with better results.

If you've developed a thinking mindset, as discussed in the last chapter, you'll find it easier to strengthen the four thinking skills. Curiosity leads to asking questions. Research is how you seek and find answers to those questions. Observation helps you notice important details. Organization allows you to sort those details into a logical order. Persistence ensures you'll stick with something long enough to figure it out. Analysis is how you figure it out. Calmness and honesty keep you focused on what the information is really telling you, so you don't get emotional or refuse to acknowledge information you don't like. Confidence ensures you will have faith in your decisions, knowing you've made the best decision you could with the information you had.

Like any other skill, you get better at thinking skills by using and improving them. Outlined below are key thinking skills, along with tips on how to strengthen them.

Research

Research is seeking and finding information.

Mention research to most people and their eyes glaze over. Research either reminds them of school term papers and libraries or makes them think of scientific, medical, or market research. But research is a skill anyone can use to find reliable information and reach better conclusions. It's a fact-finding mission. It's asking questions and then seeking answers to them. Your research doesn't have to be as rigorous as scientific research, it just has to be reliable enough to help you reach good conclusions. Whether you are trying to make a decision, solve a problem, learn something new, or achieve a goal, you can use research to improve your results.

You probably know that research can help you in your work life – although knowing it and doing it are two different things. But conducting research can also significantly improve your personal life. It can help you make better decisions regarding your health, such as checking a doctor's credentials or getting a second opinion before scheduling a surgical operation. It can keep you from being taken advantage of, such as a mechanic trying to overcharge you or an employer trying to underpay you. It can help you make smarter financial decisions, like knowing how to invest your money or whether a big-ticket item is fairly priced. It can help you with relationship issues, like researching how to set boundaries if you have high-conflict people in your life. Research can help you anytime you need more information in order to make an informed decision.

Research gives you knowledge and power. It takes more upfront time, but it saves you time, money, effort, and aggravation in the long run. Research can be the difference between success and failure.

Despite the benefits of conducting research, many people routinely fail to do it, resulting in poor decisions and outcomes. Some people don't think to do it. Some don't think they need to do it. Some don't want to take the time to do it. Some worry that they'll offend others by saying they need to do it. And others just aren't sure how to do it. Their loss is the thinking person's gain.

The type and extent of research you need to do depends on the situation. You may be able to find the information you need just by talking to a few people. You may need to research published information on the Internet or in a library, company database, newspaper, magazine, or book. If it's a business issue, you may want to conduct research by doing interviews, focus groups, or surveys. Regardless of what kind of research you do, the following tips will help you do it better.

Research Tips:

Tip #1: Conduct research based on its importance, not its convenience. The more impact a potential purchase, decision, relationship, or action will have on your life, the more important it is to do your research. For instance, the research needed when you're buying a house or forming a business partnership should obviously be more in-depth than the research needed to choose a movie or book a trip. Surprisingly, though, many people choose to do research when it's easy to do, rather than when it's important to do it. For example, online reviews are easy to find so people will often look at them for smaller purchases, like books or clothing. It's much more important to conduct research when the stakes are higher, even if it involves more work and is harder to do. For instance, if you were thinking of relocating to a different state or country in retirement, it would be worthwhile to do more than cursory research into the location. Even if you've previously visited the place on vacation or for a business trip, visiting a place is a lot different than living there. You'll want to research the factors that are important to you, such as the economy, crime rate, cost of living, climate, schools, healthcare, public transportation, the arts and culture scene, leisure activities and entertainment, and other factors that are important to you. If you're not sure where to find the information, you could check with the reference desk at your central library or do an online search for government census data and statistics for the location. If possible, you should also talk to people who live there. Since where you live has a big impact on how happy you are, it's important to do in-depth research for big decisions like this.

Tip #2: Don't let yourself be pressured into avoiding research. Your unconscious mind can cause you to do things automatically, like avoiding confrontation or trying to please other people. Unfortunately, that doesn't always work in your favor. For instance, you may fail to question an impatient doctor about your medical options or allow a pushy salesperson to pressure you into buying something you don't need or can't afford. They're not the ones who have to live with the consequences. Watch for signs that you are being pressured into making a decision before you can do your research. Some signs are obvious: "act now," "today only," or "If you value your job, you'll do what I say with no questions asked." Other signs of pressure to forgo research are more subtle. For instance, an attorney or financial advisor may imply an issue is too complicated for you to understand so you should just accept their professional opinion. A salesperson may use the *presumptive close*, in which they act like you've already agreed to buy and say something like, "Just give me your credit card, and we'll wrap this up." A friend or family member may say, "Trust me. I wouldn't ask you to invest in my new business if it wasn't a good deal for you." If you have questions, ask them. If you need time to do research before making a decision, take the time. Don't let others bully you into doing something that Future You may regret.

Tip #3: Before you start researching, clarify what you want to know or accomplish. What's the goal or purpose of your research? You can waste an incredible amount of time researching vague goals. It's ineffective to conduct broad research like, "How to improve a bad relationship" or "What are the best careers today?" Such searches are so general that you'll be overloaded with information, most of it irrelevant. Instead, think about what you really want to know or do. For instance, the search for the best careers today is useless if those careers don't match your skills, experience, or interests. A better objective might be to research what careers are best suited for someone with strong analytical and communication skills, with a bachelor's degree in business, an insurance industry background, and an interest in technology. Clarifying your goal is especially important when doing Internet research because it's too easy to waste time following links that eventually lead you far, far away from your original quest. If you clarify what you want, your research will take less time and be more targeted, relevant, and actionable.

Tip #4: Create a list of research questions. Once you have clearly determined what you want to know or accomplish, create a list of relevant questions to guide your research. Some questions will be obvious. For instance, if you're house hunting and want at least three bedrooms, an obvious question is, "How many bedrooms does the house have?" But other questions may require more thought. For instance, if you are looking for a financial advisor, one criterion you may have is that the advisor must be someone you can trust. Clearly, you won't get far if you ask prospective financial advisors, "Can I trust you?" Instead, a little preliminary online research will help you figure out the right questions to ask. For example, you might ask, "How are you compensated for your services?" to determine if there are any conflicts of interest. Make a list of specific questions you want answered and keep the list with you when you're doing your research. The list will keep you focused, and you won't get distracted by a charming salesperson, seductive web copy, or interesting but irrelevant information. You'll be able to stay on point, which will make your research more effective, efficient, and accurate. By creating a list of questions in advance, you'll also know when to stop researching. Sometimes continuing to gather additional information is just a form of procrastination. When you have gathered enough information to answer your research questions, stop researching.

Tip #5: Verify the reliability of research sources. You can't believe everything you hear or read. Your powers of observation will come in handy here, so watch for verbal, nonverbal, and written cues to determine if you can rely on the information from the source. Does it sound credible? What is the background or expertise of the source? Is the information current or outdated? Sources of information may have biases or ulterior motives that do not align with what's best for you. The admonition to "consider the source" is applicable. For instance, if you are thinking of surgery, you might want to look beyond the information on the surgeon's website. A governmental agency or nonprofit organization may be a good place to look for additional information, such as whether the surgeon is certified or whether there are potential side effects for a medical procedure. The same is true for doing business research. If you're looking to hire an employee or freelancer, they're obviously going to present themselves in the best possible light. To get a more complete picture, research any weaknesses, which you may find from checking references, reviews, social media, or other sources. Remember that we are all self-interested. That doesn't mean everyone is trying to take advantage of you, but it does mean that people are more motivated by their own interests than yours. Assume they're looking out for their interests, and you need to look out for yours. Trust, but verify.

Tip #6: Use diplomacy and tact when interviewing people. When your research involves interviewing people, either formally or informally, your people skills become critically important. You want people to open up to you, and they're only going to do that if they feel comfortable talking to you. Be sensitive and nonjudgmental, especially when you're dealing with a difficult issue. If you want people to be honest with you, you must earn their trust. Be upfront with them about how you're going to use the information they give you and keep your word. Be kind, fair, and objective. During the interview, listen more than you talk. Additionally, be observant enough to follow where the conversation leads if it is going in a direction that is relevant but that you had not anticipated when you put together your research questions. If you care about what people are telling you, they're more likely to tell you more. Make your interview a conversation, not an interrogation. Also, remember to pay attention to nonverbal cues in addition to what they're telling you. Their body language can tell you whether the interview is going well, or whether you need to adjust your approach.

Tip #7: Compile a list of resources for future use. Keep a list of the people, organizations, publications, databases, and other resources you discover during the research process. The list will save you time later if you need to consult with the resources again. Make notes on each resource, including pertinent information such as contact information, what information or service they provided, what fees were charged, the pros and cons of working with them, instructions for accessing their database, etc. You may also want to note any resources that didn't work out so you will know to avoid them in the future. As a side benefit, keeping a list of resources can help you become a trusted resource for others. People who connect others in their social and business networks gain higher visibility and influence than people who don't.

Organization

Organization is putting information in order.

The benefits of being organized are clear. Putting information in a logical order makes it easier to analyze and use. It makes you more productive. It increases your efficiency and effectiveness. It gives you a sense of control. It allows you to track your progress toward your goals. It saves you the time and effort of having to search for things or recreate documents you can't find. It saves you money because you don't have to pay late fees that stem from missing deadlines. It saves your relationships because you aren't inconveniencing others due to disorganization.

Despite the obvious benefits of organization, disorganization is a major issue for many people. Disorganization causes people to miss appointments, deadlines, and opportunities. It causes them to lose valuable time that could be spent more efficiently, productively, and enjoyably. It hurts their personal and business relationships because disorganization creates problems for other people. It also causes a great deal of stress for the disorganized person.

Some people believe that clutter is a major cause of disorganization. However, clutter is the effect, not the cause. Clutter occurs when people don't have a process for managing their stuff. They take in more information or objects than currently needed. Since they don't have an immediate use or place for incoming stuff, it just piles up.

Take the example of physical clutter, clothes for instance. In my book, *The Smart Woman's Guide to Style & Clothing*, I mention that in an organized closet, hangers should be about an inch apart so you can easily see all your clothes. If your closets are 100 inches wide, you have room to hang up to 100 articles of clothing. You can further organize them by garment: pants, tops, dresses, jackets, etc. And within those categories, you can sort by color, length, or season. Once you get to your 100-item limit, you don't buy a new article of clothing unless you dispose of an old one. Easy, organized, and logical, right? But that's not what most people do. Instead of buying only what they want, need, and have room for, they randomly buy whatever catches their eye. Instead of only keeping what fits their lifestyle, body, and personality, they hold on to clothes for emotional reasons or just in case they need them someday. The end result is a cluttered closet, rather than an organized one. They have no system.

The same thing happens with information, which can result in physical or digital clutter. Without an organizational system, people tend to acquire and keep too many documents just in case they need them someday. Their desks and file cabinets may be overflowing with paper documents, but they can't find what they need when they need it. Additionally, with storage capacity increasing and storage costs decreasing, it has become too easy to keep digital documents whether you need them or not. This creates information overload. You must have a system for storing and retrieving information, or you will not be able to readily access the information later. You need to decide up front what information should be kept and where to keep it.

Disorganization is caused by a lack of clarity. If you do not have a clear plan for handling information, objects, or commitments, they will pile up and overwhelm you. Or you will haphazardly stick things somewhere to get them out of sight, in a location which you may not remember later. A confused mind is an indecisive mind so disorganization can cause you to lose control over your information and affairs. Disorganization starts in the mind, and so does organization. Getting organized is literally mind over matter.

Organization Tips:

Tip #1: Be selective about what you allow into your life. You have only so much time, space, money, and attention. The best way to keep clutter from piling up is not to let it into your life in the first place. Be the gatekeeper for incoming information. Don't subscribe to emails, blogs, newsletters, or magazines you don't have time to read. Don't save a document to your computer, or print and file it, unless you have a good reason for doing so. The less stuff you have, the easier it is to organize. Unless you have a clear and compelling reason for acquiring or keeping something, don't.

Tip #2: Record all appointments and commitments as soon as you make them. You probably know people who make appointments, but then regularly cancel them at the last minute. Or people who commit to doing something, but then forget about it unless someone reminds them. It's annoying to other people, and it destroys credibility. When you make an appointment or commitment, record it at the first available opportunity. If you're a paper person, record it on your calendar or planner on the appointed date. If there's anything you need to do in advance of the date, like buy a gift for a party or conduct research on a project, add it to an earlier date on your calendar. If you're using digital tools, like online calendars or task managers, you can add alerts with pop-up reminders. By recording your appointments and commitments at the time you make them, you won't have to try to remember to do it later. You'll gain a reputation for being a person of your word who others trust, respect, and can count on.

Tip #3: Use prioritization to organize your day. Prioritization allows you to use your time more effectively. Don't organize and prioritize the unimportant. As author Stephen Covey said in *The 7 Habits of Highly Effective People*, "The key is not to prioritize what's on your schedule but to schedule your priorities." If you're not familiar with Covey's four quadrants, he suggested prioritizing based on what is (1) urgent and important, (2) not urgent but important, (3) urgent but not important, and (4) not urgent and not important. Ideally, most of your time is spent in Quadrant 2, which would include time spent on your goals and on the people and things you value most. Quadrant 1 is the highest priority but too much time spent there suggests you are putting out fires due to disorganization or a lack of planning. Quadrant 3 often includes other people's priorities and expectations, such as returning phone calls or responding to emails and other written requests for information. Quadrant 4 includes trivial activities and time wasters which should be minimized or eliminated. Assign levels of priority to your daily tasks using Covey's four quadrants or whatever prioritization system works for you. Some task managers allow you to designate priorities for tasks using numbers, letters, or color coding. You can use similar methods with a paper planner. By getting into the habit of prioritizing what you do each day, you'll begin to use your time more effectively.

Tip #4: Use categories to keep your digital and physical files organized. A big part of organizing information is putting it into categories to make it easier to use, file, and retrieve. In a simpler world, you would have broad, non-overlapping categories, and all subcategories would fit neatly under one of the broader categories. Your filing system would be clear, complete, and concise. A place for everything and everything in its place. But we don't live in a simple world. We are not only inundated with information, but much of it is not reducible to clear-cut categories. Such is reality. You can deal with it or just file everything under "miscellaneous." But please don't. You can simplify the categorization of information by focusing on how you received it, how you will use it, and how you can quickly find it again when needed.

The easiest method of categorization is to label a file or file folder based on how you received it – i.e., who it came from. This works well for documents you receive regularly. For example, you can file bank statements under the name of the bank and electricity statements under the name of the electric company. You can use the same categories whether your files are physical or digital.

Sometimes, it makes more sense to categorize information based on how you will use it. For instance, if you have an upcoming business trip, you might want to name the file based on the city, state, and date for the trip. You can then keep everything that pertains to the trip in that file – itinerary, flight information, documents related to the purpose of the trip whether created by you or others, etc. That way you'll have everything you need for the trip in one place.

Generally, the most logical category is the one that will help you find the information quickly if you need it again later. Choose your category based on keywords which are meaningful to you. Don't rely on your memory. Current You may think you'll remember where you put the information later, but Future You will have slept since then. Choose keywords for file names that will make sense later even if you don't remember where or when you got the information or how or why you used it originally. For instance, if you documented how you fixed a website issue, you're more likely to find the information later if you put it in a file folder named "Website Issues" than if you filed it under the name of the project you happened to be working on when the issue occurred. If documents are worth keeping, put them in a file category where you'll be able to easily find them later. Otherwise, why bother keeping them at all?

Tip #5: Take good notes. Taking good notes is an essential organizational skill, which starts with thinking about your objective. What are you going to use the notes for? In a learning environment, the objective for taking notes may be to help you understand the material and study for tests. In a business setting, the objective may be to document what was discussed, what decisions were made, what the next steps are, and who is responsible for follow-up actions. Be clear on your goal and let that guide your note-taking. Don't just document everything said; focus your note-taking on the information that is most relevant to you and your reason for being there. When taking notes, start by putting identifying information first: the date, time, location, participants and their contact information, and a brief description of the purpose of the event you're attending. Keep notes short but descriptive. Use keywords and phrases, rather than complete sentences. Underline or highlight the most important information, such as any follow-up actions you or others need to take after the event. Afterward, read your notes and summarize key points and any open items. Per Organization Tip #2, immediately record follow-up tasks you are responsible for on your calendar. Then file the notes in a logical place where you can easily find them later if needed.

Tip #6: Use tools to keep you organized. In addition to using paper or digital calendars and planners, you can also use other tools to help you stay organized. Choose the simplest tool to get the job done. Sometimes simple index cards with labeled dividers (A-Z, 1-31, etc.) can be a good organizational tool for small bits of information, such as organizing research notes, or for times when you only need information temporarily. A task manager is another helpful tool for keeping track of one-time and recurring tasks. A password manager helps you securely store all your passwords in one place. You can also find note-taking, file-sharing, and project management tools to help you stay organized. The most popular tools are easily found through an online search. In addition to specialized organizational tools, don't forget general organizational tools like email systems. For example, if you regularly send emails to a group of people, you can create a group name in your contact lists and then add individuals to the group. Next time you send the group an email, just type in the name of the group instead of adding one email at a time or hitting "reply to all" from an old, possibly outdated, list.

Tip #7: Create and maintain organizational systems. The hardest part of getting organized is getting started. Your time is limited and being organized might sound great but getting there, not so much. Some strategies make getting organized easier, and they all involve setting up systems.

One strategy is to build one small organizational system at a time. Just pick one small area in which you'd like to be more organized and create a simple organizational system. For instance, if you use a digital calendar, you can add birthdays and anniversaries to your calendar once, set them up to repeat annually, and schedule pop-up reminders a few days in advance. This simple system will ensure you'll never forget important recurring dates again.

Another strategy is to set up one aspect of a larger organizational system and then continue to build on it over time. For example, if your email inbox is overflowing, there are many things you could do to get it under control. You could unsubscribe from all promotional emails or blogs except the ones you regularly read. You could set up a separate email address and use it when you have to give out an email address but don't want to provide your personal or work email – so all your "junk mail" goes to one address and doesn't clutter up your primary inboxes. You could flag important or time-sensitive emails as soon as you read them, so they remain highly visible in your primary inbox. You could archive emails that are not currently active but which you may need later, such as for documentation purposes. You could clear out your inbox once a week. You could set up a system to automatically delete older emails after a set period of time. Rather than set up an email system all at once, you could work on one aspect at a time until you came up with a complete system that works for you. Then you could just refine it as needed going forward.

Another strategy for setting up an organizational system is to pick a cut-off date and only organize information going forward, rather than also trying to organize all your existing information. For instance, when I got a new laptop, I set up new (and more logical) file folder categories that I wanted to use going forward. I transferred over important file folders and their contents from my old personal computer, but I renamed the folders by adding "from prior PC" to the end of the name and made them subfolders under the appropriate new file folder. That way, I did not have to go through all my old files, but I still had easy access to them. Over time, when I needed to use or update an old file, I retrieved it from the subfolder named "from prior PC" and moved it into the appropriate place in my new organizational file system. I now have an effective new system and rarely need to retrieve old files.

You can make setting up systems less time-consuming by creating and refining them over time, rather than trying to set aside time to build an entire system from scratch. Also, as you're setting up organizational systems, think like a minimalist – the simpler your system, the easier it will be to maintain.

Analysis

Analysis is making sense of information.

Analysis is the skill most closely associated with logical thinking. It is studying something – like a problem, opportunity, situation, or subject – in order to understand it better. It includes looking for patterns and connections. It is interpreting what something means or how something works. Analysis allows you to make sense of information so you can use it to make good decisions.

Analysis begins with questions...Who has been impacted by this problem? What are the facts surrounding this issue? When did the situation arise? Where did the problem start? Why didn't we figure out what was going on sooner? How are we going to fix this?...and ends with answers.

The type of analysis needed depends on the situation. Descriptive analysis is analyzing data to figure out *what* is happening. Causal analysis is analyzing data to figure out *why* something is happening. Predictive analysis is analyzing data to figure out *what is likely* to happen in the future. Regardless of the type of analysis you're doing, all analysis is just the thought process you go through to figure out what the facts, your observations, and your experience are telling you.

When you analyze information, think like a detective. Search for clues. Analysis can't be reduced to a formula, but perhaps the following detailed example can illustrate the process of continuing to analyze a situation until you figure out what is going on.

When I was a vice president in the insurance industry, I was tasked with analyzing the expense structure of an insurance company that our parent company had recently acquired. Since I was more familiar with our expense structure, I began my analysis by comparing their expenses to ours. The two companies were structured differently, so I reorganized the data so I could compare expenses by function and department. The companies were also different sizes, so I looked for ways to put them on an apples-to-apples basis, like adjusting for volume so I could look at costs on a per-unit basis. For instance, when I analyzed claims department expenses, I assumed that since we processed 10 times more claims than they did, our cost to run our claims departments should have been 10 times higher than theirs. But that's not what I found. On a cost-per-claim basis, their expenses were higher than ours which suggested they were less efficient at processing claims. But I needed to dig deeper before reaching a conclusion regarding their productivity. I next began to compare our claims departments to theirs by expense category: salaries, software, travel, postage, etc. This analysis showed that "salaries" was the expense category causing most of the variance between actual and expected expenses. I continued my analysis by contacting the head of their claims division to try to understand their salary levels. Was the issue the number of people they employed? Or was it how much they were paying their employees? And was there a reasonable explanation for the higher salary expenses? The discussion with the department head answered some of my questions but didn't resolve the issue of why they needed so many people. I requested access to employee reports that showed headcounts by month for each department in the claims division. The reports provided a breakdown of regular hours worked, overtime hours, vacation hours, etc. And that's when I had the breakthrough in my analysis. When I added up the cumulative amount of vacation time for all departments in the claims division, the total amount of vacation time exceeded the maximum amount possible even if every single employee had taken the maximum amount of time off allowed by the company. To make a long story slightly shorter, it turned out that the department head had been loaning out employees to other departments and hiding their hours worked in the vacation expense category. The (former) executive had falsified the employee reports to cover up the fact that they had more employees on staff than they needed to process claims. (Please note that the name of the department and some of the other facts were changed to simplify the example and to protect the identities of the people and company involved.)

A key point of the above story is to illustrate that analysis requires persistence. If something doesn't make sense, keep digging until you're clear on what is going on. I have been told I have the tenacity of a pit bull because I won't let go until I find answers. If the analysis you're doing is important, I recommend that you be tenacious, too. Rather than accepting what you see or hear at face value, look for the proof. Only when you have completed a thorough analysis of a situation are you in a good position to decide what to do about it.

Analysis Tips:

Tip #1: Clarify the goal for your analysis. By clarifying your goal, you can narrow the scope of your analysis and save yourself time and energy. What are you trying to accomplish? If you are simply trying to understand something better, then your analysis only has to be deep enough to satisfy your curiosity. If your analysis will drive an important decision, then your analysis should be more thorough and should be focused on achieving the end goal. For instance, in the insurance company example, I knew that the reason I was asked to analyze the expenses of the acquired company was so that we could determine if they were being run efficiently. My analysis would be used to decide if any changes should be made to increase productivity, and I kept that in mind during my analysis. Part of clarifying the goal is also factoring in the importance of the analysis. If the analysis will help resolve a minor issue, it doesn't deserve much time or effort. However, if the analysis will help address a chronic problem or an issue that will significantly impact your personal or professional life, then it deserves more thought and analysis.

Tip #2: Start with what you know. Once you're clear on the goal for your analysis, write a summary of what you know so far about the issue you're analyzing. What are the relevant facts? What are your opinions? What are the observations of others involved in the situation? What data or documents do you have to help you conduct your analysis? If you're missing any information needed to do your analysis, where might you find that information? What questions are you trying to answer through your analysis? If you're not sure where to start, write down the relevant who, what, when, where, why, and how's of the situation. Then use the facts, combined with your observations and experience, to begin your analysis.

Tip #3: Look for patterns. When you're analyzing information, look for patterns in data and connections between things. What are the common denominators? What events or results appear to repeat on a regular basis? What existing or emerging trends do you notice? What similarities do you see in the circumstances surrounding an issue or recurring problem? For instance, in the nineteenth century, a doctor named Ignaz Semmelweis was trying to figure out why so many women were dying after giving birth in the hospital where he worked. His analysis showed that five times more women died in the hospital ward staffed by doctors than in the ward staffed by midwives. He looked for patterns and discovered a connection between doctors who did autopsies and patients who died in childbirth. As it turned out, the deaths were occurring because doctors weren't washing their hands before delivering babies, so they were transferring germs from cadavers to the women giving birth. Since midwives didn't do autopsies, fewer of their patients died in childbirth. When doctors started washing their hands, the death rate of new mothers dropped significantly. All because one doctor looked for patterns to explain what was causing the results he was seeing. Recognizing patterns gives you insight into cause and effect. A single point of data or an isolated incident may not mean much, but a repeated pattern may point to a root cause. If you know what causes something, you can do something about it.

Tip #4: Look for anomalies. When you hunt for anomalies, you are doing the opposite of looking for patterns. You're looking for something that stands out because it *doesn't* fit with what is normal or expected. You're looking for differences instead of similarities. Remember back in elementary school when you would be shown several items and asked, which one doesn't belong? Like a square, a triangle, a circle, and a chicken? You're looking for the chicken. What irregularities do you notice? For instance, if you suspected that one of your employees was embezzling funds, you might look for anomalies to see if you could figure out who it is. Is there a particular employee whose behavior has recently changed? For example, have you noticed a change in their demeanor? Are they working odd hours? Are they spending money more extravagantly than normal? Spotting anomalies allows you to determine if there might be something going on that is worthy of further research and analysis.

Tip #5: Look for what's missing. It's easy to become so focused on what's in front of you that you fail to question what's missing. Since looking for what's *not* there isn't something we instinctively do, you have to consciously seek it out. When you are thinking about a difficult issue that you haven't been able to resolve through other means, ask yourself: What am I not seeing? What is missing? What should be here that isn't? What should have happened that didn't? In the mystery, *The Adventure of Silver Blaze*, Sherlock Holmes figures out who stole a racehorse from the barn because of what *didn't* happen. The dog in the barn didn't bark, which meant the dog had to have known the horse thief. In your analysis, you're looking for the dog that didn't bark.

Tip #6: Come up with a hypothesis. A hypothesis is a proposed explanation used as a starting point for your analysis. A hypothesis isn't always necessary. Sometimes, you can just look at the facts and search for patterns, anomalies, or what's missing, and your analysis of the data will give you a clear picture of what's going on. You just follow the information trail. However, there are other times when you have limited information to go on. In those cases, coming up with a hypothesis, or guess, as to the root cause of an issue can give you the starting point for your analysis. For example, if your teenager suddenly becomes distant but tells you nothing's wrong, you don't have much to go on. You may then hypothesize about what could be going on. Are they hiding something from you because they know you'd disapprove? Could someone be bullying them at school or online? Does their behavior have something to do with a new love interest? Come up with your best hypothesis and then start working on proving or disproving it through further research and analysis. Just make sure you verify your hunch and don't just jump to conclusions.

Tip #7: Keep asking and answering questions. The way you analyze anything is to keep asking questions. What is this? What else could it be? What does this mean? What else could it mean? Why is this happening? Why else might this be happening? Who is involved? Who else might be involved? How does that work? How else might that work? What? What else? Why? Why else?

Who? Who else? How? How else? As you get to each answer, test your assumptions. Is it true? How do you know it's true? Persistence and flexibility are key factors in analysis. When you begin your analysis, you don't know where it will take you. But if you stick with it and follow where your analysis leads, you'll eventually find answers. Continue to ask questions and seek answers, and you'll figure out what you need to know to achieve your goal, solve your problem, or understand your situation.

Decision-Making

Decision-making is choosing what to do with information.

Until a decision is reached, nothing happens. The best research, organization, and analysis in the world is of no value until it is put to use. All conscious thinking is aimed at a goal. What are you trying to accomplish? You must decide how you'll use the information you've gathered to achieve your goal. What are you going to do?

One major obstacle to decision-making is the fear of being wrong. You probably know indecisive people, possibly even you at times. If you find yourself thinking you need more information or time, even when you've had plenty of both, you may be stalling due to the fear of making the wrong decision. If that's the case, remember the old saying, "Don't worry about making the right decision. Make a decision, then make the decision right."

Another obstacle to decision-making occurs when you don't really want to do what your analysis of a situation clearly indicates you should do. Like fear, this obstacle is an emotional one. For instance, you may have a friend or employee that you know you need to let go. They may be negative, dishonest, incompetent, lazy, or any number of other things that cause problems for you and others. Yet, you keep finding excuses for not cutting your ties. You've known them for a long time, or you feel sorry for them, or you worry it will be awkward because you belong to the same social circles. The right thing to do is not always the easy thing to do. The longer you wait, the harder it will be to make the decision, and the more damage will be done. What will you wish you had done later? Do that now. Face the consequences and get them over with.

Besides emotional reasons, another major reason for indecisiveness is that multiple options look attractive, so you're having trouble picking just one. Or none of the options appeal to you, so you're procrastinating on choosing any of them. You've looked at the facts and reasoned through your options, but you're still undecided. In that case, the tips below can help you make a decision.

Decision-Making Tips:

Tip #1: Put yourself in the right frame of mind before making a decision. If you have an important decision to make, avoid making it when you are emotional. Rarely will that work in your favor. Even if time is limited, take a moment to calm down. Breathe. Make a rational decision so you will not have to live with the consequences of an irrational one. It's especially important not to make a rash decision in anger. Decisions made in anger are usually aimed at other people and are much more difficult to undo than other types of bad decisions. If it is fear, worry, or doubt that is keeping you from making a decision, remind yourself that you can fix the decision later if needed. If you make a rational decision based on the best information available, that's good enough. Others will respect you for being decisive, and you'll become more confident in your decision-making. So, put yourself in the right frame of mind, and then make the best decision you can based on what you know.

Tip #2: Determine your decision criteria. Your decision criteria are the guidelines or requirements your decision must satisfy. Create a prioritized list of what is most important to you relative to your goal. What does success look like? For instance, your decision criteria for buying a home might include your preferred location, price, size, style, and number of bedrooms and bathrooms. Your decision criteria for choosing new business software might include the cost, the amount of time needed to install it, the return on investment, and the ease of learning and using the new software. Creating decision criteria will make it easier to choose your best option, since it allows you to compare all potential options to the criteria and only consider those that meet most, if not all, of your criteria.

Tip #3: Narrow your options to a maximum of three. This will simplify the decision-making process. We think we want unlimited options, but we really don't. It's overwhelming. If you are trying to decide between a long list of options – colleges to attend, career change options, businesses to start – start scratching options off your list. Ask yourself questions to determine what to delete: Does this option meet my top criteria? Is this an option I've already tried before? Do I have the time, money, and other resources to make this option work? Does this option rely on luck to work? Is this option in alignment with my values? Do I find this option compelling? How risky is this option compared to other options? Do the rewards of choosing this option outweigh the risks? After analyzing your options, narrow them to your top three choices if there's not one clear winner. Don't worry about the fear of missing out. Consider each option as if it were trying out for your fantasy football team. Who are you going to keep? Who are you going to cut?

Tip #4: Consider how Future You will feel about your decision. You can improve your decision-making by predicting what will happen if you choose an option you're considering. Once you've narrowed your options, take one option at a time and imagine you've chosen that option. Picture having made the decision; now how do you feel about it? And how do you think you'll feel about it a week, month, or year from now? You can't know how the future will unfold, but just by thinking about it, you are taking a longer-term perspective. Sometimes a decision looks attractive right now (usually because it's the easiest one to implement), but it doesn't sound as good when you project it into the future. Other times, it's the opposite. The decision doesn't sound as attractive right now (usually become it requires more work or is likely to upset some people), but later you will wish you had made that decision. There will be future consequences to your decisions, so think about which consequences you will prefer later. Where do you want to be? Which option will get you there? Choose that option.

Tip #5: Take a break before making an important decision. Being decisive is a great life skill, but there is a difference between being decisive and being impulsive. Making a decision in haste just to get it over with is not conducive to success. If you have already spent a great deal of time on research and analysis, you may be exhausted by the process and just want to wrap things up. However, if it's an important decision, it is worth taking a break between the collection and analysis phase and the decision-making phase. Ideas sometimes need time to percolate, and conclusions sometimes need time to be drawn. You may be well versed in your subject, problem, or issue, but need more time and space for your unconscious mind to assimilate what your conscious mind has processed. For example, authors often take a break between writing and editing so we can see our words with fresh eyes. You may need to do something similar. Take a break. Do something fun or relaxing. Work on something else. Sleep on it. Then come back refreshed and make your decision.

Tip #6: Assess your feelings *after* you make your decision. In Tip #4, you projected how you thought you would feel *if* you made a decision. In this tip, you're no longer imagining how you would feel. You've made the decision. Now how do you feel? If you feel good, at peace, or relieved, then you've likely made a good decision and can begin to act on it. But if you have a sinking feeling that you've made a mistake, stop. Question your feelings. Are you just experiencing fear because you committed to a decision or direction? Or do you know in your heart that you made the wrong decision for the wrong reasons? Years ago, I was the maid of honor for a friend and was helping her decorate the church for her wedding. I looked over at her, and she was sitting there quietly looking miserable. We talked, and she said she didn't want to get married. She had known for quite some time that she didn't want to marry her fiancé, but the plans had been made, invitations had been sent, and she felt like backing out would be letting everyone down. Despite her feelings, she stuck with her decision and married him anyway. It was an unhappy marriage that ended in divorce years later. Assessing your feelings after making a decision is not about second-guessing yourself. It's a final gut check to make sure the decision you've made is the one you really wanted to make and not one that you talked yourself into.

Tip #7: Document the reasons for your decision. When you make a decision, it's important to take the time right then to document why you made it. That is how you get better at making decisions, and at making them quicker. You may think you'll remember why you decided to do something later, but you probably won't. Remember the outcome bias, in which we judge a decision by its outcome rather than the quality of the decision at the time it was made. This can be deadly to your future decisions because it fails to consider the impact of other factors, like luck. For example, if you decide to invest in a stock because you think the company has superior management, you should note that. If you don't, and the stock goes up for a totally different reason (like because the entire market went up), then you are likely to think you made a great decision. This can cause you to make poor future investment decisions when the market is down. If you had documented your reasons, you wouldn't be fooled. You'd be able to see that the market was up 10% and so was your stock, so your return was average. Good to know. Don't quit your day job. You cannot learn to make better decisions if you don't go back and critique your decisions after the fact. And to do that, you need to know *why* you made the decision in the first place. Don't rely on your memory. If you do, you may fall victim to another bias we discussed – the egocentric bias, in which you recall the past in a self-serving manner that makes you look better. Feels good but doesn't help you.

The four thinking skills of Research, Organization, Analysis, and Decision-making are critical to thinking more effectively. By strengthening these four skills, you will be on the R.O.A.D. to winning *The Thinking Game*.

Chapter 5:

Using Effective Critical and Creative

Thinking Techniques

"To find yourself, think for yourself."

—attributed to Socrates

A thinking technique is an efficient way to carry out a mental task. You can think of these techniques as tools to prompt better thinking. Thinking is hard work. Thinking techniques make the job a little easier.

The thinking techniques that follow can be roughly divided into two camps: critical thinking techniques and creative thinking techniques. Critical thinking is rational, analytical thinking based on knowledge. Creative thinking is a new way of looking at things based on imagination. For example, if you wanted to publish a book, critical thinking might involve analyzing what other successful authors have done to write, publish, and market their books. Creative thinking might involve visualizing a new way of publishing a book like Michael Hart did in 1971 when he invented the ebook. Achieving your goals requires a combination of critical and creative thinking.

What makes these techniques effective is that they give your mind a starting point and direction. Thinking is not a paint-by-number kind of thing, but the techniques give your thinking some structure. When you're drawing a blank, or your mind is spinning, or you're overthinking, you can use the techniques to help focus your thought process. These techniques will also help you get around faulty beliefs, biases, and emotions that can cloud your judgment.

Experiment with these thinking techniques to determine which ones are best suited to your style and situation. You'll quickly find that some are a better fit than others. You'll also find that you can sometimes get better results by combining two or more techniques.

Critical Thinking Techniques:

A simple online search will reveal that there are numerous critical thinking techniques you could try: Analytical Hierarchy Process, Decision Matrix Analysis, Multi-Attribute Utility Theory, Paired Comparison Method, and more. The problem with these techniques is that they are complex, so most people won't use them. The critical thinking techniques listed here are easy to understand and use. They will help you think clearly, solve problems, and make better decisions.

Pros-and-Cons List

When you are making a yes-or-no decision, a pros-and-cons list can be very effective. They're also simple to use. They help you to be more rational and less emotional. By thinking through the pros and cons, you are less likely to leave out critical factors that affect the quality of your decision.

You probably make pros-and-cons lists in your head all the time. When you find yourself thinking, "Well, on the one hand,…but on the other hand…," you are mentally making a pros-and-cons list. Next time try writing it down. Your mind can only hold so many pieces of information in short-term memory. Writing down the pros and cons makes it easier for you to see arguments for and against a proposed course of action. Writing down the list also makes it easier for you to evaluate important decisions later because you'll have a record of the reasons for your decision.

As you make your list, focus on the factors that matter most to you. A pro is not a pro if most people would think it is a benefit, but you don't care about it.

Also, avoid duplicate items on your list. If you're trying to talk yourself into, or out of, a course of action, you may unconsciously try to stack the deck. To avoid biasing your decision, make sure each item is unique. For instance, instead of including three cons like (1) it's too expensive, (2) I can't afford it, and (3) I'd have to buy it on credit; just note one con related to cost.

To be most effective, a pros-and-cons list should be weighted or prioritized. It's not just a numbers game. You want to make the best decision possible. If you have fewer pros, but they are significant and the cons are trivial, then weight the pros more heavily.

The pros-and-cons technique is best for yes-or-no decisions, not for comparing multiple options. For instance, it helps you make decisions like: Should I accept this job? Should I retire now? Should I downsize? Should I join this group? Should I volunteer for this charity? Should I raise my prices? Should I sell my business?

If you get in the habit of making pros-and-cons lists, you will automatically make better decisions because you will be thinking about the most important factors. For example, if you have trouble saying no or feel like your time is not your own, this technique can change your life. Instead of automatically saying yes to all invitations or requests, you can take a minute to jot down the pros and cons before responding. Should I accept the invitation to this event? Pros: My friend asked. I'm free that night. Cons: I don't want to go. It would be my first free night in 3 weeks. I'd rather spend some time at home with my family. The event is expensive. The event is an hour's drive from me. I would not get home until after midnight and I have to work the next day. You get the picture. A simple pros-and-cons list causes you to check in with yourself and consciously decide what you really want to do instead of responding on autopilot.

Checklists

Using checklists is a great technique for routine tasks and decisions. Checklists free up memory and minimize your chances of forgetting something important. Setting up a checklist requires some thought on the front end, but it saves you time, effort, and aggravation on the back end.

An example of a helpful checklist is one that prepares you for trips. Before your next trip, take a minute to note the things you need to do before you travel – put a hold on the mail, get extra cash, turn down the thermostat, unplug the coffee pot, etc. Also, make a packing list. You can start by including the things you always take, such as a phone charger, laptop, prescriptions, toiletries, passport, pajamas, etc. If you frequently travel, you might want to add additional sections to your checklist such as what to pack for different climates, types of activities you'll be doing, and for business versus pleasure trips. If you create a travel checklist, you will save time and won't have to worry about forgetting things on future trips.

Checklists are also helpful at work. They are ideal when there are many steps in a process. A checklist will ensure you don't forget a step when you're distracted or in a hurry. Pilots and doctors use such checklists because a missed step could have critical consequences. Use checklists when it's important that you complete multiple steps, especially when the steps must be completed in a specific order. For instance, if you work in accounting and are responsible for closing the books at month-end, you might want to prepare a checklist for all the steps in the closing process.

Checklists are also helpful to remind you of essential stuff. These are not step-by-step checklists; they are lists of the most important things you need to remember. For instance, if you're a professional photographer, your checklist for a shoot might include making sure your camera battery is charged, that you have a back-up battery, that your lighting gear is packed, that your memory card is not full, etc. If you've ever made a stupid mistake at work because you forgot something basic but important, a checklist can help.

You can also use checklists for making decisions. These aren't things you need to do, they're things you need to think about or consider. For instance, you might want to create a checklist of the biases we discussed earlier so you can review the list before making big decisions. Another example of a decision-making checklist would be putting together a list of interview questions for use during the hiring process to ensure you ask the same questions of every candidate.

Since thinking takes so much energy, it makes sense to use checklists whenever possible. They are especially helpful for things that are important or recurring. Put thought into the initial checklist, make modifications as needed, and then forget about it until you need it again. You'll get more done in less time by using checklists. They're a great hedge against forgetfulness, distractions, and emotions. They'll remind you of what you need to do even when your mind is somewhere else.

+1 Solutions

Another technique to improve your thinking is "+1 Solutions." Dr. Jason Selk, a mental toughness coach, coined the term to remind his clients to take things one step at a time. A +1 solution is an improvement to the current situation that brings you one step closer to a full solution. The idea is to make incremental improvements.

Trying to find the *perfect* solution can be counterproductive. It puts too much pressure on you to get it right the first time. Instead of helping you come up with the best solution, it can paralyze you with indecision. The end result: no solution. It's far more productive to focus on finding a *better* solution. If you knew the perfect solution, you would have already implemented it. As Albert Einstein reportedly said, "We can't solve problems by using the same kind of thinking we used when we created them."

Every problem has a solution. Otherwise, it's not really a problem; it's something you don't control and can't do anything about. But even solving actionable problems may require multiple steps. The +1 Solutions technique helps you take the first step, then another, and then another. When you see that you're making progress, you'll be motivated to keep going until you accomplish your end goal.

Instead of aiming for big, sweeping changes, try making incremental improvements. You are less likely to resist making small changes, so they are easier to implement. They are also easier to undo if they don't work out as expected. They allow you to learn as you go. If you want to make a major change, you may not know how to do it. With +1 Solutions, you don't have to know. You just need to think of one thing you can do differently to make the situation better. Do that. Then think of one more thing and do that. Repeat until you're satisfied with the outcome.

For instance, if you wanted to become financially secure, you could use +1 Solutions to help you achieve your goal. Instead of trying to come up with the perfect plan to become financially secure, you could tackle one issue at a time. For instance:

- **First +1 Solution:** Analyze your current expenses by tracking your spending habits for a month (e.g., track purchases made with cash, checks, credit, or other forms of currency).
- **Second +1 Solution:** Look for expenses you can eliminate, like magazines you never have time to read anyway.

- **Third +1 Solution:** Think about where you can reduce expenses, like switching to lower-cost service providers for mobile devices or car insurance.
- **Fourth +1 Solution:** Explore ways to increase your income, such as working more hours, getting a promotion, or starting a business on the side.
- **Fifth +1 Solution:** Research ways to increase your savings and investments, such as allocating more of your disposable income to savings, switching to a bank that pays higher interest rates, or taking full advantage of your company's 401(k) plan.

You can also use the +1 Solutions technique when you are creating something. For example, if you have to write a report or give a presentation, you might start with a blank page and write down everything you know about the topic. That's your starting point. Then look back over what you've written and start editing it to make it better. If there are gaps in your knowledge, conduct research and analysis to bridge the gap. If you re-read what you wrote and it still needs improvement, continue to make incremental changes until you're satisfied with the final report or presentation. By using this rough-draft mentality, you take the pressure off yourself to make it perfect the first time. Your starting point is just the first draft; keep improving it until you like the final result.

5 Whys

The 5 Whys technique helps you get to the root cause of a problem. The technique was developed by the founder of Toyota Industries and was used to identify the root cause of problems in the company's manufacturing process. The concept is simple. You state the problem and then ask why it is happening. When you come up with a reason, you then ask why *that* is happening. You continue to drill down on your answers five times until you get to the root cause of the problem. The number 5 is arbitrary, but the idea is to keep asking why until you get to the real problem, not just additional symptoms of the problem.

The reason many people don't achieve their goals is that they put up with recurring problems. They complain about them, but they don't do anything to address them. They know *what* the problem is but fail to get to the root of *why* it is happening. They know there's a problem, but they don't think they can do anything about it or aren't willing to take the time to figure out what to do about it. Problems persist because they are never fully addressed. The hope is that they will just go away on their own. After a while, the problems are just accepted. If you can identify what is causing a problem, you are halfway to solving it.

If you have a problem, ask yourself why the problem is occurring. Keep asking until you get beyond the obvious answers. Here's an example of how the 5 Whys technique might work:

Problem: I don't have enough money.

Why #1: Why don't you have enough money?
Answer: Because my company doesn't pay me enough.

Why #2: Why don't they pay you enough?
Answer: Because I'm already maxed out at my pay grade.

Why #3: Why are you maxed out at your pay grade?
Answer: Because I can't move up to another pay grade without a promotion.

Why #4: Why can't you get a promotion?
Answer: Because getting a promotion requires getting a certification.

Why #5: Why can't you get a certification?
Answer: Because I don't want to take the training required to get the certification.

This person might frequently complain about money but blame it on their employer for not paying them enough. However, if they honestly used the 5 Whys technique, they would realize the real reason they don't have enough money is that they aren't willing to take the training to get the certification that would get them a raise in pay. If they continued the 5 Whys process, they might discover they don't want to take the training because they're afraid they'll fail. Now, we're back to the impact of negative emotions arising from the unconscious mind. If they faced their fear, they would realize there was no downside to taking the training. If they passed, they'd get a raise. If they failed, they'd be no worse off than before. But they'll never reach that conclusion unless they keep asking themselves why they don't have enough money until they get to the root cause.

Of course, many problems have more than one root cause. For instance, in the prior example, the person's spending habits may also add to their money problems. If you use the 5 Whys technique in conjunction with the +1 Solutions technique, you can address one root cause at a time and then move on to the next one.

Comparison Table

Creating a comparison table can help you decide between multiple options. It makes it easy to see how your different choices stack up against one another. Comparison tables are commonly used for comparing similar products or services. For instance, when shopping for a new coffeemaker, you may see different models listed by column and different features or attributes listed by row. Then, for each model, you'll see a checkmark if it has a given feature, or you'll see data to describe a given attribute, such as size, number of cups, etc.

You can use this same concept when you're trying to choose between multiple options. Create a simple table. List your options by column and your desired features, benefits, or criteria by row.

A simple example is creating a comparison table when you're in the market for a major purchase, like a new car. Across the top, you might list four sports utility vehicles (SUVs) you're considering: Honda, Ford, Mazda, and GMC. In each row, you might list features or criteria that are important to you: Price, Miles Per Gallon, Sunroof, Heated Seats, Reverse Sensing System, etc. Then just fill in the table with the data you find after researching each SUV. You can then compare each option and choose the one with the features you most desire.

Creating a comparison table is a great way to compare multiple options. All the data is right there in front of you to help you make the best decision. It is much easier to compare multiple options feature by feature than it is to analyze one option at a time and then try to remember which one had which features. It also keeps you from falling prey to the recency effect bias which can cause you to weigh information on the last option more favorably than earlier ones since the last option is freshest in your mind. Comparison tables help you get around cognitive biases and emotions that may lead you to make impulsive decisions you may come to regret.

The prior example was to help make a purchase decision, but you can use comparison tables to compare any options – cities you might want to move to, career choice options, freelancers you might want to hire, etc. Just put your options in columns and your decision criteria in rows. Any time you're trying to choose between multiple options, think about whether a comparison table can help you make the best choice. Just remember that comparison tables work best when you are comparing apples to apples, so use this technique when you are choosing between similar options.

Six Thinking Hats

The Six Thinking Hats technique helps you clarify your thinking by looking at issues from multiple perspectives. This technique was created by Dr. Edward de Bono to help teams solve problems, make decisions, and explore new ideas. He came up with a system of looking at issues from six different perspectives. You put on each of the six different thinking hats to approach a situation from different angles. By doing so, you get a more complete picture and make better decisions.

- The White Hat is neutral and focuses on facts and figures.
- The Red Hat is emotional and acknowledges how you feel about an issue.
- The Black Hat is cautious and identifies risks and points out weaknesses.

- The Yellow Hat is optimistic and identifies upsides and rewards.
- The Green Hat is creative and looks for new ideas and opportunities.
- The Blue Hat is organized and manages and integrates the other perspectives.

While the Six Thinking Hats technique is primarily used in business, it can also be used to make better personal decisions. Looking at issues from multiple perspectives improves the quality of your decision-making and gives you more balanced, well-rounded solutions to problems. It's like having six different experts weigh in on an issue.

This technique is especially helpful in overcoming biases that stem from your natural way of looking at things. For instance, if you are emotional by nature, you may automatically look at things from a Red Hat perspective. By deliberately looking at things from the other five perspectives, you will make more rational decisions. Or if you tend to see things from a Yellow Hat perspective, putting on your Black Hat can remind you to also look for potential risks to your strategy so you can find ways to mitigate them.

Here's a simple example of how you might use the Six Thinking Hats technique to make a decision regarding whether to go back to school to get a master's degree. With your White Hat on, you might gather facts about potential schools, cost of tuition, prerequisites, when the next term starts, etc. With your Red Hat on, you may acknowledge that you are excited but also fearful, because you've been out of school for a long time. With your Black Hat on, you might think of the downsides to going back to school – taking on student debt, the time needed to study and attend classes, missing out on social activities and spending time with your family, etc. With your Yellow Hat on, you might think about how going back to school would help your career and earnings potential. With your Green Hat on, you might look for creative ways to pay for school or find a way to combine two dreams, like moving to your dream city and attending school there. With your Blue Hat on, you could organize your research on the schools, summarize the main points of what you discovered, and decide what you want to do after taking all perspectives into consideration.

Creative Thinking Techniques:

Whereas critical thinking techniques help you think more logically, creative thinking techniques help you think more imaginatively. As Albert Einstein wrote, "Imagination is more important than knowledge. For knowledge is limited, whereas imagination embraces the entire world, stimulating progress, giving birth to evolution."

Meditation

Meditation is a technique for focusing your mind. Because of all the chatter that goes on in our heads, it can be difficult to think clearly. A regular practice of meditation can allow you to quiet your mind, so you can think clearly, calmly, and creatively. If you read biographies of successful people, you'll find that many successful entrepreneurs, athletes, and celebrities meditate. People like Oprah Winfrey, Ray Dalio, Michael Jordan, Arianna Huffington, Paul McCartney, Tony Robbins, LeBron James, and Clint Eastwood regularly meditate because it works.

There are many types of meditation. Some people prefer a form of mindfulness meditation. With this practice, you focus on your experience in the current moment rather than allowing your mind to wander. This is a great way to develop your powers of observation. By paying attention to what's happening around you instead of getting lost in your thoughts, you'll see things you've never noticed before. You'll observe details and make connections that will allow you to come up with more creative ideas. A great benefit of mindfulness meditation is that it can be done anytime, anywhere.

Loving-kindness is another common form of meditation. It is also sometimes called Metta meditation. The goal of this meditation practice is to cultivate feelings of love and kindness toward yourself and others. Loving-kindness meditation reduces stress and positively impacts your relationships. During this practice, you send positive messages to yourself, people you know, and the collective peoples of the world. For instance, one Buddhist practice consists of silently thinking, "May I be happy. May I be peaceful. May I be free of suffering." Then you repeat the same mantra for other people. The idea is to start with your loved ones and continue moving outward to other people, even those with whom you have a difficult relationship. Keep repeating the mantra until you experience a feeling of peace. Loving-kindness meditation puts you in a more positive frame of mind, so it is a good practice to do before interacting with others. It also frees you from negative feelings which can hijack your mind and stifle creative thinking.

Another popular form of meditation focuses on breathing. This focused attention on the breath calms your mind and frees you from anxiety and overthinking. It improves your concentration, so it is especially helpful to practice when you really need to focus. The practice itself is simple, but simple doesn't mean easy. You put all your attention on your breath. When thoughts or feelings arise, you observe them and let them pass away without engaging with them. In this relaxed state, more creative thoughts may bubble up, including the solution to a problem you've been trying to solve.

There are other forms of meditation as well. Progressive relaxation helps you release tension in your body. Zen meditation helps you explore your spirituality. Transcendental meditation focuses on a mantra and promotes self-realization. Research and explore different types of meditation until you find what works for you.

You can even make up your own meditation practice. For instance, when I was in the process of writing this book, I came across an article that said psychoanalyst Sigmund Freud kept a statue of Athena on his desk. Athena was the Greek goddess of wisdom. Despite also being the goddess of war, she came to personify wisdom, peace, and prosperity. Athena was a powerful figure in the epic poems *The Iliad* and *The Odyssey* by Homer, who wrote about how Athena provided guidance and aid to heroes on their journeys. Greek philosopher Plato believed Athena symbolized *mind* and *intelligence*, possibly even *divine intelligence*. So the goddess Athena was on my mind one day when I ran into an issue while working on *The Thinking Game*. No amount of critical thinking was helping me figure it out, so in exasperation, I closed my eyes and said, "OK, Athena, how would *you* resolve this issue?" I wasn't really expecting a response, but I got one anyway, and it solved my problem. Maybe we all have the wisdom of Athena within our unconscious minds. All I know is that sometimes when I'm not sure what to do, I ask a question, meditate on it, sometimes sleep on it, and frequently get an answer sooner or later. Try calling on a higher wisdom and see if it works for you or come up with your own meditation practice.

Visualization

With the visualization technique, you form a mental image of something you want to happen. Since your unconscious mind cannot distinguish between reality and perceived reality, it will accept the visualization as if it were true if you repeat it frequently enough. If you convincingly imagine what you want to see happen, your unconscious mind will push thoughts and impulses into your conscious mind to help you figure out how to make it happen.

Visualization has been used in many situations, especially in sports. Basketball players imagine themselves making their free throws, golfers envision themselves making their shots, and football players picture themselves making touchdowns. If you envision yourself succeeding, you increase your chances of success.

The visualization technique that works for athletes can also work for you. For instance, if you have to give a presentation, you can visualize yourself giving a great speech. Think about the best speakers you've ever seen, in person or on video. What makes them great speakers? Picture yourself with those same qualities giving your own presentation. See yourself speaking confidently and having the impact you desire. The more feeling and detail you put into your visualization, the more convincing it will be to your unconscious mind.

Visualization is like writing, directing, and starring in your own movie. You are the hero, and there is something you want. Don't just picture the end result you want. There is rarely a "happily ever after" in a movie until the hero overcomes a challenge. So picture yourself doing the things you would need to do to successfully overcome challenges and achieve your goal. The more convincing you make your script, the more likely your unconscious mind will help you produce in reality what you visualized in your mind. Imagine as many details as you can to support what you'd like to have happen. Feel the emotions you would naturally feel, such as excitement, pride, or confidence. Don't limit your imagination to what Current You is capable of achieving. You are in the process of becoming, so visualize the Future You that you aspire to become.

Affirmations

Affirmations are a close cousin to the visualization technique. With visualization, you are working with images. With affirmations, you are working with words. Professional boxer Muhammad Ali noted, "It's the repetition of affirmations that leads to belief. And once that belief becomes a deep conviction, things begin to happen."

Many people try affirmations and conclude they don't work. And, they're right. Affirmations don't work if you repeat meaningless words by rote as if you were memorizing information for a test. That's why it is often ineffective to read books that provide affirmations for health, wealth, and happiness, and then just repeat those affirmations. They are not your words. They are unlikely to resonate with you unless you and the author are kindred spirits. Come up with your own words. If you think in terms of money, not finances, then use the word *money* in your affirmations. If you think in terms of a lover, not a significant other, then use the word *lover* in your affirmations.

Also, be mindful of what you do and don't control. An affirmation to find a new love is fine but specifying that you want it to be your coworker who is clearly not interested in you is a waste of time. Aim high but be flexible. Leave room for your unconscious mind to work its magic. Things don't always show up exactly as you expect. What's important with affirmations is that they clearly reflect what you want in your life.

Finally, create affirmations based on what you'd like to have happen *and* what you are willing to work to make happen. Forget about the power of attraction and the ability to materialize things out of thin air with no effort on your part. That may happen in virtual reality, but not in this reality. Affirmations plus action will help you achieve your goals.

Brainstorming

Brainstorming is a technique for generating creative ideas and solutions to problems. Start by formulating a goal or question for the brainstorming session and then write down every idea or answer that comes to you. Brainstorming allows you to temporarily ignore your rational mind, so it does not stymie your creativity. Later, you can use critical thinking techniques to vet your ideas and figure out how to implement the best ones. During brainstorming, you're just looking for new ideas and lots of them.

When you brainstorm, you will often find that the first thoughts you come up with are obvious and predictable. For instance, if you're trying to solve a problem, you may generate ideas that are similar to what you've tried before. After you run out of the usual suspects, you'll start to think of more creative ideas.

While brainstorming, avoid judging the merits of your ideas. That would be like editing a novel as you write it. It will stifle your creativity and the flow of ideas. Because you are generating ideas off the top of your head, many of them will be bad ideas. So what? You only need one good idea. But before you can come up with Número Uno, you will most likely need to come up with números dos, tres, cuatro, cinco, seis…and so on.

After your brainstorming session, you can go back and start scratching ideas off your list. Focus on eliminating duplicate ideas and those without merit. If an idea addresses an aspect of the problem but not the whole thing, keep it on the list. Remember +1 Solutions. You can always combine ideas and then flesh out a workable solution.

Mind Mapping

Mind mapping is a more visual form of brainstorming. With brainstorming, you generate a list of as many ideas as you can, as quickly as you can, in no particular order. Mind mapping is a brainstorming technique that graphically organizes your ideas into categories and subcategories. It allows you to focus on the relationships between ideas rather than on disconnected, random thoughts. You can do it on paper or use mind-mapping software.

To draw a mind map, start by putting your main topic (which can be a goal, idea, problem, opportunity, issue, etc.) in the middle of the page. Then draw lines from the main topic to each subtopic underneath it. Then repeat the process adding additional lines to subtopics of your subtopics.

For instance, suppose you were thinking of starting a new business but weren't sure what you wanted to do. You might create a mind map by writing *New Business* in a circle in the middle of the page. Off that circle, you might draw lines to ideas for types of businesses you might want to start, such as *Consulting Services* or *Organizational Products*. Then you would add additional ideas. For instance, off of *Organizational Products*, you might add lines branching out to *Planners*, *Calendars*, and *Journals*. Then off of *Planners*, you might add lines for *Digital Planners*, *Printed Planners*, *General Planners*, *Specialized Planners*, etc. Your map could go off in multiple directions, and you could continue to drill down as additional ideas came to you in each area.

Brain Mining

Brain mining is a creative problem-solving technique proposed by Theodore Scaltsas, a philosophy professor at the University of Edinburgh. With this technique, you search your mind for old solutions that you can apply to new kinds of problems or issues.

Scaltsas noted that if you're working on a difficult problem, you can solve it by redefining the problem until it resembles one you have solved in the past. You do this by imagining that the conditions blocking your progress are lifted one by one until you produce a version of the problem that resembles a problem you've solved before.

He gives the (rather extreme) example of being in a room on the tenth floor with a fire raging outside the door. Normally you would assume you can't open the door to escape because of the fire. You can't jump out the window to escape because you're too high up. Either option would be fatal. But what if you remove the assumption that you can't jump out the window and instead assume that you can safely do so. How might you do that? Your mind might come up with the idea of a parachute. Then you might look at the window curtains in the room in a different light. Maybe they could be turned into a parachute so you could safely exit the room.

New business ideas often arise from the brain mining technique. For instance, my favorite corkscrew is the Screwpull wine opener now manufactured by Le Creuset. It was invented by Herbert Allen, who worked in the oil and gas industry. He applied his problem-solving skills and oil industry background to invent an easier way to open wine bottles. The Screwpull he invented removes the cork from a wine bottle using a similar process to how oil rigs use rotary drilling equipment to remove oil from the ground. Different problem; same solution.

When you're trying to solve a difficult problem, look for ways to use an old solution for a new problem.

Critical thinking techniques help you think logically and ground you in reality. These techniques allow you to learn from the past and use your observations and experiences to achieve what you want in the present. Creative thinking techniques help you use your imagination to think differently about what is possible. These techniques can keep you from limiting yourself to the past and help you create a better future.

Together, critical and creative techniques can help you achieve your goals, solve your problems, and experience better results. They help you reimagine your life and then figure out how to make it a reality.

Chapter 6:

Questions to Frequently Ask to Improve Your Thinking

> *"Everything in the universe is within you.*
> *Ask all from yourself."*
>
> —attributed to Rumi

Thinking is just asking and answering questions. It is that simple and that complicated. Simple because we all know how to ask and answer questions. Complicated because we do not always do it well. To think successfully, you must know the right questions to ask and then figure out how best to answer them. The thinking mindset, skills, and techniques covered so far will help you think better. So will asking better questions. The most important questions are those you ask yourself. Asking questions is not a trivial pursuit. It's not about asking inconsequential questions like what sounds good for dinner; it's about asking yourself the deeper questions that determine your quality of life.

Many people don't know what they want because they never make it a priority to find out. Asking yourself questions is the only way to figure out what you need in order to have a satisfying life. And you can't just ask once and expect to receive meaningful answers. You must continue to drill deeper to get past your surface wants and discover your root needs. The other reason you must continue to ask yourself questions is that what you want changes over time. As you learn, grow, and mature, your desires will change. What you want at 65 will be different from what you wanted at 21.

Businesses put together lists of *Frequently Asked Questions* because those are the questions their customers most want answered. To make the most of your life, create your own list of *Questions to Frequently Ask*. These are the questions you most want answered because they will have the biggest impact on your success and satisfaction in life.

The *Questions to Frequently Ask* process includes 4 steps:

1. Identify the important areas of your life
2. Develop questions to ask yourself in each of those areas
3. Ask and answer the questions at designated times set by you
4. Act on your answers

Start by identifying the most important areas of your life. What do you value and how do you spend your time? One area everyone should include is Success. You must define what success means to you. It does not have to agree with the cultural definition of success, which currently includes some version of fame and fortune. For most people, the other major life areas will include Relationships, Work, Money, Health, and – for many people – Spirituality. Another area everyone should include is Personal Satisfaction. Beyond that, the important life areas will vary from person to person. Yours will depend on what else you value. In the sample *Questions to Frequently Ask* that follow, I have included Fun, Learning, and Achievement as examples of additional important life areas based on values.

After you've chosen your important life areas, develop a set of questions to ask yourself periodically. You can use the questions I have provided or come up with your own.

Success

Having a definition of success around which you can build your life leads to a life that feels cohesive and meaningful. Think about what success means to you and allow it to guide your decisions and actions in all areas of your life. Ask yourself:

1. What is my definition of a successful life?
2. Based on that definition, am I more successful now than I was a year ago?

3. Am I spending my time in ways that are contributing to a successful life?
4. What is one change I could make that would help me become more successful?
5. Am I willing to put in the time and effort to make that change?

Relationships

When answering the questions about the people in your life, think of your personal and professional life. Anyone who occupies a significant amount of your time or thoughts should be included, even if it's someone who is no longer in your life. Ask yourself:

1. Who are the most important people in my life?
2. How is my current relationship with each of these people?
3. If there are issues with anyone, what is one thing I could do to address them?
4. Are there any people I should be spending more (or less) time with?
5. Am I being the kind of person who attracts the kind of people I want in my life?

Work

For most people, work refers to a paid activity. However, work is any physical or mental activity you do to achieve specific results. So if you are retired, a volunteer, a stay-at-home parent, or a hobbyist, you can modify the questions to suit your definition of work. Ask yourself:

1. Is the work I'm doing satisfying and meaningful to me?
2. Am I doing my work to the best of my ability?
3. Is there a different type of work I would rather be doing?
4. Is there a different place I'd rather be doing my work?
5. What is one thing I could do to improve my success and satisfaction at work?

Money

When thinking about money, focus on your definition of success. Answer the questions in a way that reflects what *you* value, not what others value. Ask yourself:

1. Am I spending money on things that matter to me?
2. Am I earning enough to support my idea of a successful life?
3. Am I saving enough money to maintain a cushion for unexpected events?
4. Am I investing wisely to achieve financial security?
5. What is one thing I could do to improve my financial position?

Health

Taking care of your health gives you the energy to take care of other things and other people in your life. If you take your health for granted, it may leave you someday. Ask yourself:

1. How is my overall physical and mental health?
2. How might I improve what I eat, drink, and think?
3. How might I improve my level of exercise and movement throughout the day?
4. Am I using meditation or other mindfulness practices to improve my mental health?
5. What is the most important change I could make to improve my health?

Personal Satisfaction

Your answers to these questions will have a big impact on your success in every other area of your life. Inner truth matters more than outward appearances. Ask yourself:

1. How do I feel about myself and my life right now?
2. Do I need to focus more on positive feelings: joy, love, gratitude, inspiration, serenity?
3. Do I need to focus less on negative feelings: fear, worry, envy, anger, doubt, anxiety?
4. What is one trait I can work on that would help me feel better about myself?

5. What is one habit I could change that would improve my personal satisfaction?

Fun

However you define success, it should include time to relax and have fun. There is a time for seriousness and a time for play. A satisfying life requires both. Ask yourself:

1. What is something I enjoy doing just for the fun of it?
2. How can I make routine activities more fun?
3. Who are the people in my life that I have the most fun with?
4. How can I change my mindset to see the humor in life?
5. What time wasters could I eliminate to free up some time for play?

Learning

One of the major reasons people lose interest in life is because they stop learning and growing. Their thoughts and actions become old and stale. They become bored and boring. If you want a fulfilling life, you must continue to learn throughout your life. Ask yourself:

1. What books have I read lately that gave me new insights?
2. What new skills have I recently acquired that can help me with my work?

3. What is something new I've recently learned about someone in my life?
4. What do I know today that I didn't know yesterday?
5. What is something that interests me that I would like to learn more about?

Achievement

We are goal-oriented beings. Our achievements set us apart from other species and are part of what makes us who we are. We were born to evolve. Progress is in our DNA. Ask yourself:

1. What goals would I most like to achieve?
2. What decisions do I need to make?
3. What problems do I need to address?
4. What opportunities interest me?
5. Which goal do I want to pursue next?

You can create your own set of questions to prompt your thinking on the most important areas of your life. The best time to come up with your questions is when you are in a contemplative mood. Also, it's not necessary to come up with all your questions at once. Pick an area of your life you want to improve, and then challenge yourself to come up with questions that will prompt positive changes in that area. Keep track of your questions and answers in a physical or digital notebook.

If you make it a habit to regularly ask yourself questions like these, you will begin to see better results in all areas of your life. Find a frequency of asking and answering questions that works for you. It may vary based on what's going on in your life. For instance, if you have good health habits, you may only need to ask yourself questions about your health every quarter to make sure you stay on track. However, if you are currently experiencing problems at work, you may need to ask yourself work-related questions more frequently. At a minimum, you should ask yourself all of your questions at least once a year.

Finally, remember to act on your answers. Until you do, nothing will change. The answers to your *Questions to Frequently Ask* can be the basis for the goals you set...which will be the focus of Part Three.

Bonus: Emotional Self-Awareness Questions

Asking and answering questions about the major areas of your life is important and acting on them is how you create a great life. If you can also discipline yourself to ask emotional self-awareness questions, you will significantly upgrade your thinking and results in all areas of your life. Emotional self-awareness is the ability to recognize your emotions and understand why you are feeling them.

Practice identifying your emotions as they arise. Whenever you experience a heightened emotional state, take a moment to identify what the emotion is (e.g., fear, anger, or anxiety) and why you are feeling it. If you immediately question yourself, you may find that you're just tired or hungry. Or your defenses are down because you're not feeling well. Or you are feeling more sensitive than normal for other physical or emotional reasons. Figure out what's really going on, and then you can ask yourself questions to keep your emotions from adversely influencing your thoughts and actions.

When you're emotional and are about to say or do something you know you shouldn't, ask yourself:

- What are the possible consequences if I say or do this?
- Will I regret saying or doing this later?
- What can I do now to avoid saying or doing anything until I can think calmly and clearly?

When you're irritated over something minor or petty, ask yourself:

- Why am I getting so upset over this?
- Will I even care about this a week or month from now?
- What can I tell myself to put this in perspective and maintain my peace of mind?

When you can't make a decision, ask yourself:

- Why am I being so indecisive?
- What's the worst thing that can happen if I make the wrong decision?

- If I weren't afraid of being wrong, what decision would I make?

When you're procrastinating, ask yourself:

- Why am I avoiding doing this?
- What benefits will I receive if I take action?
- How can I motivate myself to take action now?

When you're worrying about something, ask yourself:

- Is my worry accomplishing anything besides making me feel bad?
- Do I have any control over this?
- If there's something I can do, am I willing to do it?

When you're not feeling confident, ask yourself:

- How is feeling insecure helping me in this situation?
- What's the downside to acting confident even if I don't yet feel it?
- What would I do right now if I were feeling confident?

The above are just examples of common situations where you may unconsciously react because of heightened emotions rather than consciously responding in a rational manner. Discover your hot buttons and design your own set of emotional self-awareness questions. The trick is to get in the habit of taking a minute to *think* so you can respond mindfully. The more you ask these kinds of questions, the more quickly you will be able to shift your thinking in a positive direction in the future. You are in control of your thoughts, feelings, words, and actions, but you must choose whether you will assume that control.

In Part Two, we talked about how to improve your conscious thinking. In Part Three, we'll discuss how you can use conscious thinking to help you achieve specific goals. We'll talk about the 4-step process for achieving your goals, which includes using the right process to (1) set your goal, (2) create your plan, (3) take action, and (4) analyze your results.

Part Three:

Applying Conscious Thinking to the

4-Step Process for Achieving Your

Goals

Chapter 7:

Step 1: Set the Right Goal

"When it is obvious that goals cannot be reached, don't adjust the goals, adjust the action steps."

—attributed to Confucius

In Part Two, we talked about all the things you can do to improve conscious thinking. You can change your mindset. You can develop or strengthen your thinking skills. You can practice effective thinking techniques. You can get in the habit of regularly asking and answering questions. Now that we've covered how to improve conscious thinking, it's time to apply that knowledge in Part Three. Thinking that doesn't lead to action leads nowhere. The object of *The Thinking Game* is to achieve a goal. You have the power to choose your own goals, and that is the path to personal freedom.

A goal is anything you are trying to do or achieve:

- A result you're trying to get
- A target you're trying to hit

- A problem you're trying to solve
- A decision you're trying to make
- An opportunity you're trying to obtain
- An issue you're trying to resolve
- A habit you're trying to change
- An experience you want to have
- A contribution you want to make
- An object you're trying to acquire
- A game you're trying to win
- A situation you're trying to manage
- A purpose you're trying to fulfill
- An advantage you're trying to gain

In short, a goal is your objective. What do you want?

Most people spend very little time consciously thinking about goals. If they have any goals at all, they generally fall into one of two categories. They are either personal goals related to health; e.g., My goal is to lose 15 pounds. Or they are performance goals related to work; e.g., Our department's goal is to cut expenses by 10 percent. Rarely does the average person consciously set other types of goals. They may have other things they want, but they don't think of them as goals, so they don't create plans to achieve them.

Other people think they have goals: My goal is to start my own business someday. My goal is to write a book. My goal is to make more money. My goal is to meet someone new. These are not goals; they are vague wishes with no plans for their fulfillment.

Some people don't believe they have time to set goals, which is sad. If you are not setting goals, you are just reacting to everything happening around you. You are not proactively directing your life. Your life is running you, rather than the other way around. Setting goals puts you in charge. Goals are how you move forward in a direction chosen by you. Without goals, you will scrabble to find meaning. Unless you set goals and get serious about achieving them, you will always feel like something is missing in your life: a purpose.

The biggest obstacle to goal-setting isn't a lack of time, it's a lack of clarity. Setting a goal requires you to think about what you want, which was the purpose of the last chapter. Until you consciously set a clear goal, you can't commit to it. Until you commit to it, you can't create a plan to achieve it. Until you create a plan to achieve it, you can't take definitive action. Until you take definitive action, you can't get results. In other words, nothing will happen.

Criteria for Goals

Setting the right goal is more important than achieving the wrong one. By putting more thought into defining your goal, you will save yourself wasted time and effort. The right goal is one you care about achieving. It's a goal that is aligned with one or more of your values.

For example, if learning is one of your core values, then choosing to master a new language could be the right goal for you. If you instead choose a goal based solely on the expectations of others, then achieving it will not bring you much satisfaction because it isn't a goal you care about.

To significantly increase your chances of setting and achieving the right goal, your goal should meet the following criteria:

Criteria #1: Your goal should clearly indicate what you want and why.

A clear goal specifies exactly *what* you want and *why* you want it. The *what* and the *why* are equally important and should be considered jointly. One without the other is insufficient. Together, they ensure you set the right goal for the right reason. Your *what* is what you want to happen. What do you want to do or achieve? Your *why* is why you want it to happen. Why does the goal matter to you? What's your primary purpose or reason for setting the goal? What value would achieving the goal satisfy? Your *what* will keep you focused and your *why* will keep you motivated.

Your goal should be specific. Setting vague goals to make *more* money, *improve* your posture, spend *less*, or have *better* relationships, is a waste of your time. How much is *more*? Improve how? Better in what way? A vague goal is a sign of confused thinking. Gaining clarity on a vague goal is like adjusting the lenses on your binoculars until the fuzzy vision becomes clear. Start with a general idea of your goal and then continue to refine it until the goal is clear. You gain clarity by asking questions.

Here's a simple example of how a person might clarify a vague goal:

Initial Goal: Start exercising (the *what*), because I want to lose weight (the *why*).

Clarifying questions related to the *why*:

Q: Why do you want to lose weight?
A: Because I want to be healthier.

Q: If you were able to be healthier at your current weight, would you be satisfied?
A: No, I'd still want to lose weight.

It's important to push back on your *why* because you want to find the *most* motivating reason for achieving your goal. Doing so increases your chances of sticking with the goal until it's accomplished. Sometimes your initial *why* is the reason you think you should want to do something, but it's not the real reason.

Q: Why do you *really* want to lose weight?

A: Because then I would have more energy. The extra weight makes it hard for me to climb stairs, let alone do anything more active or adventurous.

Q: If you were able to increase your energy at your current weight, would you be satisfied?

A: No, I'd still want to lose weight.

Q: So why do you *really, really* want to lose weight?

A: Because I don't like how I look. Looking in the mirror is depressing. Since my divorce, I feel like I've let myself go. For a while, I just didn't care how I looked. I knew I was eating too much junk food, but it made me feel better. And, anyway, I wasn't in a relationship, so what difference did it make? Now, I'm mad at myself for giving up on me. But now, I've put on so much weight that I just don't know how to get it off.

Now, we've arrived at the real reason the person wants to lose weight. It's clear that no matter how many secondary benefits would result from losing weight, their main reason for wanting to lose it is the impact it would have on their appearance and self-esteem.

If your *why* arouses a strong emotion, it's a good indication that you have hit on the real reason you want to achieve a goal. When it comes to motivation, emotions play a key part. Emotions are especially critical if your goal is challenging. If you don't have a strong desire to achieve your goal, you are more likely to give up on it when you run into obstacles or when it just becomes too hard. You can logically tell yourself why you *should* achieve a goal, but that won't work if you care more about something else.

Be honest about your *why* even if it feels shallow, petty, or stupid to you, or if you think it will sound that way to others. The truth will help you set the right goal. One caveat: If the truth is that there's a toxic reason for your *why* – like a desire to hurt (or get back at) someone – ditch the goal. Even if you achieve it, you'll poison your mind in the process. There are already too many bad actors dealing cards against humanity, so don't play their game.

Knowing your real *why* also helps you figure out the right *what*. You'll know that if achieving the *what* will not satisfy your *why* then it's not the right goal for you.

In this example, the goal that is most likely to lead to success is one that recognizes that the main reason for wanting to lose weight is to feel more attractive and confident. Now that we've addressed the *why*, let's move on to the *what*. In this example, the original *what* was to start exercising.

Clarifying questions related to the *what*:

Q: How will exercising help you lose weight?
A: It will help me burn calories.

The Thinking Game

Q: How many calories will it help you burn?

A: It depends on what type of workouts I do. Maybe I should focus on cardio.

Q: What kind of cardio would you do?

A: I would take an aerobics class.

Q: How many calories would you burn if you took an aerobics class?

Note that when you are asking yourself questions, you will not have all the answers. Use your research skills to find them. In this case, the person might call a local fitness center or conduct online research to find out how many calories they would burn in an aerobics class.

A: It looks like, at my weight, I could burn about 500 calories in a one-hour, low-impact fitness class.

Q: How many times a week would you take the class?

A: I could go twice a week.

Q: OK, so that's 1,000 calories a week. Losing one pound of body fat is the equivalent of 3,500 calories. So, you would be losing one pound every 3.5 weeks. Is that what you want to do?

A: No. It will take me forever to lose any appreciable weight at that rate.

Q: How else might you lose weight?

A: Well, I guess I could change my eating habits. I could cut down on the number of calories I consume.

Q: How much weight would that help you lose?

A: Based on my research, if I cut 500 to 1,000 calories a day from my diet, I can lose 1 to 2 pounds a week. That will help me lose weight faster than working out.

In the interest of brevity, we can stop here, but the person could continue the questioning until they were clear on what they wanted to choose for their goal. Maybe they would lose all the weight through diet. Maybe they would combine cutting calories through diet with burning calories through exercise. The point is that they would continue to ask and answer questions until they arrived at a clear goal.

Here is how their goal may have changed from vague to clear based on their questions, research, and analysis:

Initial Goal: Start exercising (the *what*), because I want to lose weight (the *why*).

Final Goal: Cut 500 calories from my daily diet (the *what*) to reduce my weight by 50 pounds by one year from today so I will feel more attractive and confident (the *why*).

Note: This Final Goal includes all 3 criteria for setting goals. It is clear, as discussed in this section. It is also measurable and time-based, which will be discussed in the next two sections.

Not only was the initial goal vague, but it turned out it was not the right goal. How frustrating would it have been to exercise for a year and not get the desired results? The final goal is very clear. They now know exactly what they're trying to do, and they know exactly why they're trying to do it.

Criteria #2: Your goal should be measurable and trackable.

The next criterion for ensuring you have a strong goal pertains to measurability. If your goal is not measurable, you will not be able to track your progress toward its achievement. The ability to track your progress is psychologically motivating. You are far more likely to abandon a goal if you can't tell whether you are getting closer to achieving it.

Some goals easily lend themselves to measurability. You can measure health goals based on weight, body measurements, cholesterol levels, the results of a physical, etc. You can measure financial goals based on income, savings, spending, investments, assets, wealth, etc. You can measure work goals based on projects completed, billable hours, sales levels, revenue increases, expense reductions, profits, etc.

Assigning a number to your goal makes it easier to measure. You just need to determine which metric makes the most sense given what you're trying to accomplish. It's important to choose a metric that directly relates to your goal, not just one that's easy to measure or track. For example, if your goal were to grow your business via social media, you might be tempted to track the number of followers because that's easy to do. However, if you had a lot of followers on social media, but they were not buying from you, your number of followers would be meaningless. In this example, a more useful metric might be to measure conversion rates from social media.

If your goal is tied to a number, it's easy to come up with ways to track your progress. If you're a numbers person, you can set up a worksheet to chart your progress. For example, let's say you're writing a novel with a goal to write 1,000 words per day to complete the first draft in 90 days. Each row of your worksheet could include the date for the next 90 days: (1) January 1st, (2) January 2nd, (3) January 3rd, etc. Your columns might be (A) Daily Word Count Goal, (B) Actual Daily Word Count, (C) Actual - Goal DWC, (D) Cumulative Word Count Goal, (E) Actual Cumulative Word Count, (F) Actual - Goal CWC. Once you set up your worksheet, all you would have to do is enter your daily word count, and the formulas would do the rest. You would easily be able to see your progress. For instance, if on Day 10 your actual daily word count was 800, you'd see at a glance that you were 200 words below your daily goal. However, if your cumulative word count were 12,000 on Day 10, you'd see that you were 2,000 words ahead of your cumulative goal. Nicely done.

You can set up a similar worksheet for any kind of goal that can be tied to a number. By seeing your progress on the worksheet, you'll know whether you're on track to achieve your goal. If you are, keep doing what you're doing. If you're not, you'll have an early indicator that you need to get back on track.

If you're more of a visual or creative person, a worksheet may not work for you. That's fine. You might instead create a graphic like charitable organizations do to track progress toward fundraising goals. For instance, they may show contributors a graphic of a thermometer for a goal of raising $10 million with indicators at the $1 million mark, the $2 million mark, and so on up to the $10 million goal marked at the top of the thermometer. As contributions roll in, they may color in the thermometer in red up to the level of current donations. Then everyone can visually see the progress. You can apply this same concept to any goal you have that is tied to a specific number.

Use your imagination to come up with a tracking mechanism that works for you. Make a game of it. Achieving goals is fun, so why shouldn't tracking them be fun, too?

Some goals are harder to measure, such as those involving relationships or personal interests. Sometimes, even these goals can be tied to a number. For instance, If you and your spouse feel you don't have much time for each other because of work or children, you might jointly set a goal to have a date night once a week. Or if you have a personal hobby, your goal might be to set aside two hours a week for it. You can easily track these types of goals on a digital or physical calendar.

As you continue to play *The Thinking Game*, you'll get better at coming up with ways to measure your goals. The simpler, the better. For instance, as previously mentioned, comedian Jerry Seinfeld came up with a system for tracking his goal of working on new jokes every day. He would put a red X through every date on the calendar on which he wrote new material. His goal was to never break the chain of Xs. This is a great method to use for tracking habit goals. For instance, if you want to exercise every day, put an X on your calendar for every day you work out. It's satisfying to see an uninterrupted string of Xs that show how well you're doing.

The multitalented Benjamin Franklin also created a simple process to track his goal to regularly practice thirteen moral virtues. He created a grid with a row for each virtue and a column for each day of the week. Although he would focus on only one virtue at a time (such as self-control), he would put a mark by *any* virtue he violated on any given day. His goal was to eventually have no marks on the grid, which would mean he had achieved his goal of strengthening all thirteen virtues. This method also works well for habits you're trying to break. For instance, if you were trying to stop smoking, you might put a hash mark on your calendar or planner for each cigarette you smoked each day. Your goal, of course, would be to eventually see no marks on your calendar, which would mean you had dropped the habit.

You can use these methods for tracking your progress toward your goal or use creative thinking to come up with your own method. The important thing is to think of effective ways to measure your goals, and then track your progress toward their achievement.

Criteria #3: Your goal should be time-based.

If goals are not time-based, it's too easy to procrastinate. There's no deadline so you can convince yourself you'll get around to accomplishing your goal later. That's like the bar sign that says, "Free beer tomorrow." Tomorrow never comes.

Both achievement goals and habit goals should include time elements.

Achievement goals relate to a specific accomplishment tied to a deadline. For example, you might set a date by which you will achieve a financial goal, earn an advanced degree, visit a foreign country, or start a new business. The primary time-based components of achievement goals are when to start and when to finish.

You can also set achievement goals related to problem-solving. For instance, you may set a goal to solve a work-related problem by a certain date. By attaching a deadline, you turn solving the problem into an achievement goal. Solving a problem, especially a chronic problem, is an important achievement. If you view solving a problem as an achievement goal, you'll address the problem sooner, rather than letting it fester and turn into a major issue.

Additionally, you can set achievement goals related to decision-making. It's easy to put off making a decision when you're fearful or uncertain, but indecisiveness doesn't get you results. Put an end to indecision by setting deadlines for making decisions and then sticking to them. For small decisions, decide immediately. For more important decisions, allow more time, but just enough to do your research and analysis. Making a decision is a major achievement because it leads to action, which leads to results, which leads to feedback, which leads to better decisions.

Habit goals relate to specific actions you want to change. It may be a habit you want to start, like exercising, meditating, or speaking up at work. Or it may be a habit you want to break, like overeating, worrying, or interrupting when others are talking.

For habits you want to start, the time-based components include when you'll start, how frequently and for how long you'll practice the habit, and what time you'll practice the habit. For example, if you wanted to start exercising, you might set a goal to walk for 30 minutes, every weekday, starting at 6 a.m., beginning the following Monday.

For habits you want to break, the time-based elements include when you'll start working on breaking the habit and when you'll make exceptions. For example, if you wanted to eliminate sugar from your diet, you might set a goal to stop eating or drinking anything with added sugars starting the day after your birthday, except for Saturdays which would be your cheat days.

There are many other goal-setting processes, but many are too complicated or too time-consuming so most people won't bother doing them.

Also, you may have noticed that the clear, measurable, and time-based criteria sound a lot like the S (Specific), M (Measurable), and T (Time-bound) criteria in the highly touted S.M.A.R.T. goals. Very observant of you. The problems I have with S.M.A.R.T. goals are threefold. First, there are dozens of different words and meanings ascribed to the letters in the acronym. Does the *A* mean Attainable? Acceptable? Achievable? Does the *R* mean Realistic? Relevant? Or something else? Since there's no consistency in the meaning ascribed to the letters, I don't find them particularly useful. Second, I disagree with the concept of setting goals that are *attainable* or *realistic*, because it can cause you to set goals that are easily achievable and are beneath your potential. As actor Will Smith said, "Being realistic is the most commonly traveled road to mediocrity." Dropping the *A* and *R* is the smart thing to do if you don't want mediocre goals.

Third, S.M.A.R.T. goals don't really address whether you've set the right goal. You can set a goal that is specific, measurable, attainable, realistic, and time-bound, but if the goal is not tied to something you value, it's not the right goal for you.

If you remember to set goals you care about that are clear, measurable, and time-based, you will be well on your way to winning *The Thinking Game.*

Bonus: Additional Goal Boosters

Boost the power and effectiveness of your goals with these five actions:

1. **Prioritize your goals.** Your most important goals are those whose achievement will have the biggest impact on your life. Prioritize your goals based on their importance to you, not based on which ones are easiest to achieve or most impressive to other people.

2. **Set stretch goals.** A target goal moderately improves your current results and is a good start. A stretch goal significantly improves your current results and is a great way to finish. Stretch goals force you to up your thinking game because you can't just do more of something, you must do something different.

3. **Focus on goals over which you have control.** Set goals over which you have greater control. Avoid setting goals that primarily rely on luck or other people to achieve. Instead, set goals where your own thoughts and actions significantly increase your chances of success.

4. **Put your goals in writing.** Writing down goals makes them more real to you. It also makes it more likely that you'll achieve them. Put them where you'll see them every day and personalize them. Write them in calligraphy. Type them in a bold font. Put them on a colored index card. Include them on your screensaver. Or do something else to set them apart from your everyday notes and documents.

5. **Commit to no more than three major goals at a time.** You only have so much time and energy. If you jump from goal to goal, you will dilute your power and effectiveness. Concentrate on a small number of important goals. Pursuing a few bold goals will have a greater impact on your success and satisfaction than chasing dozens of smaller ones.

Chapter 8:

Step 2: Create the Right Plan

"A good plan implemented today is better than a perfect plan implemented tomorrow."

—attributed to General George S. Patton

Once you've set your goal, the next step is creating a clear plan to achieve it. How will you get what you want? What's your strategy? Your plan should be detailed enough that you have a roadmap for what you need to do, but flexible enough to allow for changes during implementation. The right plan, when properly executed, will allow you to effectively and efficiently achieve your goal.

As you think about your plan, look for the most direct route to achieving your goal. The best plans are simple. Like the old aphorism says, "Simplicity is the ultimate sophistication." Simple doesn't mean easy to implement, but it does mean straightforward and easy to understand. If you make the plan too complicated, you're likely to abandon it before you achieve your goal.

When you are creating your plan, stay focused on your goal. That may sound obvious, but we sometimes start out thinking about the big picture but then get lost in the details during the planning process. We start including steps that are not critical to the achievement of the goal. We include things we're comfortable doing or enjoy doing, even if we don't really need to do them to achieve the goal. We also get distracted by things we think would be cool to do. Focus on the goal. Every item in your action plan should be necessary to achieve your goal, or it should be deleted.

Steps for Creating an Effective Action Plan

To create an effective plan for achieving your goal, work through the following simple steps. Thinking through each step will enable you to take more focused action later. You'll have a roadmap for efficiently getting where you want to go. You'll also have a record of what got you there.

Step 1: Map out a preliminary plan based on what you know.

Having clearly defined your goal, you know exactly what you want and why you want it. Now think about how you're going to get it. Start with a blank page or worksheet and map out a preliminary plan for how you might achieve the goal. What steps do you think you would need to take to achieve your goal? Don't overthink it.

Just use your knowledge and experience to create a high-level plan that includes the major steps needed to achieve your goal.

If you get stuck, use the thinking techniques we previously discussed to help you come up with your preliminary action steps. For instance, brainstorming or mind mapping can help prompt your thinking on what steps to include.

Start by focusing on the broadest, most important aspects of the plan. For example, if the goal were to publish a book, the preliminary plan might include:

1. Write the book
2. Publish the book
3. Market the book

Then add additional tasks under each major component of the plan. For example, writing the book might include tasks like choosing a topic, creating an outline, conducting research, writing each chapter, etc. Publishing the book might include tasks like deciding whether to self-publish or traditionally publish, finding a publisher or agent, choosing a title, designing the cover, etc. Marketing the book might include tasks like creating a website, writing blog posts, building a mailing list, promoting the book on social media, etc. Once you've created your main tasks, add any additional subtasks that come to mind.

Think of the preliminary plan like an outline. Start with major tasks and continue to drill down to lower level tasks until you've fleshed out a preliminary plan.

Once you have a list of action items, put them in chronological order to the best of your ability. For example, in the prior example, the plan might include putting all the writing tasks first, then all the publishing tasks, and then all the marketing tasks. In reality, they overlap, but the preliminary plan is just the starting point. Your tasks may have to be moved around later, especially for tasks that are contingent upon the completion of other tasks. For now, you are just using your organizational skills to put the tasks in your plan in the order that makes the most sense to you.

Step 2: Research your knowledge gaps.

When you look at your preliminary plan, you may notice two types of knowledge gaps. First, you may not know what tasks should be included in parts of your plan. Second, you may not know how to complete the tasks that are in your plan. You can close your knowledge gaps with research.

First, conduct research on what additional tasks to put in your plan. If the goal is one you've attempted before or is in an area in which you have a great deal of expertise, you may already know what tasks need to be done. In that case, you can skip this part, because you will have already included the necessary tasks in your plan. However, If you are unfamiliar with what it takes to achieve the goal, you may need to do some preliminary research to figure out what tasks to include in your plan. For example, a first-time author may not know the steps in the publishing process. If your research shows you left off any major steps, add them to your preliminary plan. At this stage, you are doing just enough research to complete your plan. Your focus is on what you need to do, not on how to do it.

Second, schedule time to research tasks you don't know how to do. You are not going to stop to do that research now, you are just going to schedule it into your plan. Think of it as just-in-time research. For example, in the author example previously discussed, the author may have included advertising as a task, but not know where or how to advertise. In that case, they could simply add a task such as *research paid advertising options* in the appropriate part of the plan. You can do the same thing with tasks you know you need to do, but which will require future research to learn how best to do them.

In Step 2, you are making use of the +1 Solutions thinking technique. You started out with a preliminary plan in Step 1 and are now improving the plan after doing additional research or scheduling future research into your plan.

Step 3: Figure out timing and assign dates to the tasks in your plan.

If you're working on an achievement goal, you should have already determined your start date and deadline during the goal-setting process. The time between the start date and deadline is what is *potentially* available to achieve your goal. Look at your calendar and see what else you have going on between your start date and your deadline. Also, allow time for the unexpected. Now you know how much time is *really* available to achieve your goal.

With your calendar in front of you, look at your plan and start assigning dates for when to begin each task. Work backward from the deadline. So, if you think the last task on your plan will take two days to complete, assign it a date of at least two days before the deadline. (You should probably include a cushion. Remember the planning fallacy from our bias list, which is underestimating how long it will take to complete a task.) After that, assign a date to the next-to-the-last task depending on how much time you think it will take. Continue this process until you've assigned a date to all of your tasks.

At this point, you will be giving your deadline a reality check. If all the tasks fit comfortably into your schedule, congratulations. If not, you have some rethinking to do. First, determine if the deadline is flexible. If it is, you can push back the deadline to fit the tasks. For example, if you worked back from the deadline with your tasks and determined that to get everything done, you would have needed to start two weeks ago, you can just push your deadline back two weeks and adjust the dates for the tasks accordingly.

However, your deadline may be firm. Maybe it is tied to some external event or was set by someone else. If your deadline is not flexible, you can review your tasks to determine if any of them can be changed, scaled back, deleted, or handled more quickly. Use your analytical skills to figure out how to modify your tasks to hit the deadline without compromising the goal.

For example, I was once asked to complete an insurance company forecast in a fraction of the usual time. My team was stressed and correctly pointed out that, even working long hours, we'd never be able to complete our usual in-depth forecast by the expedited deadline. I agreed and suggested we follow our usual process for forecasting the most critical components of the forecast – such as premium revenue and claims – but use shortcuts for everything else. For instance, for fixed costs like administrative overhead, we could just use our historical averages and run rates to forecast expenses and make adjustments for known variances. For variable costs, we could make estimates based on the drivers for each category of expense. For example, we would normally calculate commission expenses at the lowest level of detail based on numerous factors like line of business, distribution channel, first year versus renewal year, etc. and then sum up the results. In the absence of time, we could instead look at actual commission *rates* and apply those *percentages* to forecasted premiums to get forecasted commissions. Modifying our tasks worked. We met the deadline and when we later completed the full forecast, it confirmed that our scaled-back forecast using high-level analysis had worked well to project results.

In addition to modifying your tasks, you can also consider using additional resources to help you complete your tasks in a more timely manner so you can meet your deadline. Resources will be covered in the next step.

When you've finished your analysis, modify the tasks and their assigned dates in your plan.

You've probably heard that what gets scheduled gets done, and it's true. If all you do is make a note of the deadline for a goal without scheduling interim deadlines for the major tasks needed to complete it, you are likely to miss your deadline. Or you may rush through the remaining tasks and compromise quality. Or you may give up on the goal altogether. None of these are desirable outcomes.

Assigning dates to the individual tasks on your plan allows you to check your progress at any time. All you have to do is look at your plan to see if you have completed all the tasks up through the current date. If you have checked them all off, carry on. If you haven't, you'll know what you need to do to catch up. That's a less stressful way to achieve even the most challenging goals.

So far in this step, we've been talking about achieving goals with a deadline. If you're working on a habit goal, there is no deadline, but you'll still want to figure out timing. When you set the goal, you would have already determined your start date, how frequently you'll practice the habit, and when you'll practice the habit. Now you can look at your calendar at the start of each week to see if there are any conflicts. If there are, you can decide to skip practicing the habit on the days you have a conflict, or you can schedule a make-up day. For instance, if you were planning to run every weekday but have a conflict on some days, you can schedule make-up days on the weekends. The more consistently you practice a new habit, the more quickly it will take hold, so you're better off making up missed days rather than skipping them.

Step 4: Determine what resources are available to you.

While creating your plan, think about what resources are available to help you accomplish the tasks in your plan. If you leverage your resources, you'll be able to get more done in less time. Major resources to consider are time, money, and knowledge.

Time. Consider all the ways you can leverage time to carry out the tasks in your plan. First, think about how you can free up more of your own time. Are there any activities you can eliminate or scale back to allow more time to work on your goal? Also, consider technology. Is there a software application that can save you some time? For example, if your plan included setting up a budget, you might want to use one of the free budget templates available online instead of creating a budget from scratch. Second, think about whether other people can contribute their time and effort. Can you delegate any of the work? Are there people you know who would volunteer to help out? Time is a valuable resource, so consider how best to leverage it.

Money. Depending on the goal, you may be able to use money as a resource. Could you outsource any of the tasks in your plan? Outsourcing makes sense if you can hire an experienced person or business to handle a task for you at a reasonable price. Paying someone to do a task that requires expertise you lack, that takes time you don't have, or that involves work you don't enjoy doing, is a good use of outsourcing. Just be sure you use your research skills to find the right resource and pay the right price for their services. Additionally, make sure you build adequate time into your plan for the hiring process and for reviewing outsourced work.

Knowledge. In addition to your own knowledge, think about people you know with expertise related to your goal or to the specific tasks in your plan. Identifying knowledgeable people and asking them questions can shorten your learning curve and help you achieve tasks quicker. If you don't know anyone with the information you need, reach out to your personal and professional connections to see if they know someone. You can also acquire helpful information by consulting published materials, such as blog posts, how-to videos, magazine articles, and books. These resources can help you achieve your goal more efficiently and effectively.

Once you have determined what resources are available to you, incorporate them into your planning.

Step 5: Anticipate potential challenges or obstacles.

In this step, you will look over your plan to identify potential challenges or obstacles. The challenges could be due to other people, circumstances, resources, or even your own emotions or habits. Consider how you might overcome these challenges if they arise and modify your plan as needed. For instance, if you know that someone you are relying on to complete a task always turns things in late, you may want to give them an earlier deadline than your real deadline.

You may also want to consider if-then planning for tasks that are critical to the achievement of your goal. If-then planning just means that *if* X happens, *then* you will do Y. It's a backup plan. So for the most critical elements of your plan, think about alternative actions you could take if it becomes necessary.

Step 6: Finalize the Plan

Once you've completed Steps 1 through 5, you're ready to finalize your plan. Review the plan in its entirety to determine if you need to make any further changes, such as adding any missing tasks, deleting duplicate tasks, or changing tasks based on new information.

Also, double-check your calendar to ensure no additional issues or conflicts have arisen since you started the planning process. And if you need anyone's signoff on your plan, now would be the time to get it.

This may seem like a lot of work, but the time you spend planning will save you time, energy, and frustration later. If you have not achieved some of your past goals, not having a plan before jumping into action may have been the issue. This is especially true for challenging goals with a lot of moving parts. Trying to achieve a goal without a plan is like trying to build a house without a blueprint. It can be done, but is it a risk worth taking?

If you follow the six steps in the planning process, you should have a plan that clearly shows what you need to do and when you need to do it. If everything looks good, you're ready to move from creating your plan to executing it.

Chapter 9:

Step 3: Take the Right Action

"The most difficult thing is the decision to act, the rest is merely tenacity. The fears are paper tigers. You can do anything you decide to do. You can act to change and control your life; and the procedure, the process, is its own reward."

—attributed to Amelia Earhart

If you've given sufficient thought to your goal and plan, you've positioned yourself to succeed. You're prepared. Now it's time to act. Setting goals and creating plans are essential thinking steps, but thoughts must be turned into action to get results. Until you test your thinking in the real world, there's no way to tell if it's effective. Until you execute your plan, it is just theoretical. It's an idea about how to achieve your goal. Only action can tell you what works and what doesn't.

Some people are great at setting goals and making plans, but they're all thought, no action. To act requires time and effort. Some people talk about their great ideas and all the things they're going to do, but they never do them. They enjoy thinking about their future success but don't want to put in the necessary work to achieve it. They are not willing to give up anything else to free up time and energy to pursue their goals. For such people, laziness and a lack of commitment are the issues.

But many times, the issue isn't laziness, it's fear. What if you fail? What would people think of you? What would you think of yourself? If it doesn't work out, what will you do? Besides the fear of failure, numerous other fears can keep you from taking action: the fear of success, the fear of criticism, the fear of running out of money, the fear of losing an important relationship, or whatever else it is that you fear. Thinking about goals feels good, achieving them feels great, but it's the time in between that can be an emotional landmine. It takes courage to conquer your fears. The fear-induced urge to avoid or postpone action can be overcome through emotional self-regulation. More on that shortly.

To guard against the tendency to postpone action, remind yourself of why your goal is important to you. Visualize all the benefits you'll receive if you accomplish your goal. What will your life look like if you achieve it? Also visualize the consequences of not accomplishing the goal. What will your life look like if you don't achieve it? Isn't your goal worth sacrificing a little comfort and accepting a little uncertainty?

Like any good action game, *The Thinking Game* has challenges, and the outcome is not assured. You execute your strategy with the goal of winning, but each goal is just one game within the bigger game of life. You can't win if you don't play. If you play, you'll either win, or you'll learn something that will help you win the next time. The only sure way to lose is not to play at all.

Hints to help you take more effective action:

All actions are not created equal. Some actions are just busywork. Your hands are busy, but your mind is idle. Some actions are halfhearted. You're going through the motions but are not fully committed. To be effective, action must be mindful and wholehearted. Actions must be directed at a specific goal with an expectation of achieving it. Following are hints on how to take more effective action.

Hint #1: Practice emotional self-regulation.

Emotional self-regulation (also known as emotional regulation) is the ability to understand and deal with your emotions. It's the ability to cope with difficult situations in a way that is emotionally mature and socially acceptable. When the inevitable setbacks occur while you're working on a goal, remind yourself to control your emotions. Remain calm and confident, and if you're not feeling it, assume the role of someone who is. This is the action step, so act. See yourself as an actor and the character you're playing as the hero in the story. All heroes face villains, and your villains include fear and all its known associates, like worry, doubt, anger, anxiety, and frustration. Don't let the bad guys win.

We like to think we're rational beings, but often our goals are derailed by emotions, not a lack of ability. When things don't go our way, we get upset. When we get upset, we can't think clearly. When we can't think clearly, we can't take effective action. When we can't take effective action, we can't achieve our goals.

So when circumstances, other people, or your own fears threaten to overwhelm you, take a breath and practice emotional self-regulation. Things happen. You can handle this. It's not a big deal. Use the creative thinking techniques we discussed, like meditation or visualization, to help you re-establish your peace of mind. Remember to pause between stimulus and response. It is worth taking time out to ensure you'll take effective action, as opposed to destructive action or no action at all.

Hint #2: Track your actions against your plan.

The plan is your action guide. It includes all the tasks you planned to do and the dates by which you planned to do them. Each task in your plan is a smaller goal that supports your larger goal. Tackle them one by one. As you finish a task, check it off. Also, note the date you completed it. That way, you'll have a better idea of how long tasks actually took versus how long you thought they would take. This will help you plan better in the future. It will also reveal opportunities for improvement. For instance, you might be able to automate a time-consuming process.

In addition to checking off tasks in your plan, document significant actions you took that were not in your plan. For example, if you had not anticipated needing regulatory approval for a work-related goal, add that additional step to the plan. The plan then becomes a living document showing all the major actions you took, not just the ones you originally planned to take.

The plan is not the holy grail. It is not sacred. The entire purpose of the plan is to help you achieve your goal. Once you start taking action to achieve your goal, you may find that the plan is flawed. Your research or results may show that a given task is not going to help you achieve your goal and may even hinder your efforts. In that case, strike the task from your plan and briefly note why you chose not to do it.

Some people can be very inflexible when it comes to sticking to the plan. When a company I worked for was acquired, we were told that the integration plan required that all new subsidiaries must switch to the same software as the parent company to ensure compatibility throughout the organization. As a result, we were told to switch from Excel to Lotus for our spreadsheet software. We pointed out that the parent company was planning to switch to Excel the following year, so it didn't make sense for us to switch from Excel to Lotus and then back to Excel again a year later. The person in charge agreed but said the plan was the plan and we all needed to get on board. Fortunately, saner heads prevailed, but that's what can happen when the plan is treated as the end goal instead of a means to the end.

Documenting your planned and unplanned actions gives you a record of your progress. It is especially helpful for goals you may wish to repeat or build on in the future. Why create extra work for yourself? If you track your actions against the plan and document any additional actions taken, you won't have to try to remember what you did later. You'll know. This will help you take more effective and efficient action in the future. Each time you set a similar goal, you can improve on what you did before.

Hint #3: Embrace trial and error.

When you created your plan, you used logic to determine the steps you would need to take to achieve your goal. When you execute your plan, you'll have to experiment to see what really works and what doesn't. If you learn to embrace trial and error, taking action will be more enjoyable and effective.

For some reason, our culture treats failure like that other F-word, something to be avoided in polite society. Why? If you take action and fail to get the results you want, take a different action. What's the big deal about trying something that doesn't work out? How else are you going to learn and improve? Failure is information. Use it to try something else, and you'll increase your knowledge about what is, and is not, effective.

The people who are most afraid of failure never come close to reaching their potential. Fear of failure stops them. But you have to realize that the more challenging your goal, the more likely you'll experience some failures on the way to achieving it. So what? If you lost a hand of poker because you made a bad call, would you refuse to ever play again? If you make a mistake, deal with it.

Remember that curiosity is part of the thinking mindset. Apply your curiosity toward figuring out why a course of action isn't working. If an action isn't working, tinker with it. Think of how you might improve what you're doing and then test it out. Experiment and see what happens. You're playing *The Thinking Game*, so keep playing until you're satisfied with your results.

If you adopt a trial-and-error philosophy, you'll be more successful. You'll also be happier because you'll be able to minimize the fear of failure that otherwise sucks the joy out of everything. Failure is not a dirty word; it's a rite of passage.

Hint #4: Take action consistently and persistently.

Depending on your goal, there may be some actions you must repeatedly take if you want to see results. If you are a writer, you must consistently write. If you are a salesperson, you must consistently sell. If you are in rehabilitation, you must consistently rehab. Sometimes the hardest part of achieving a goal is not that you don't know what to do, it's doing it. And doing it again. And yet again.

Repeating the same actions can feel like a never-ending chore, especially if it takes a long time to see results. This is especially true for habit goals. You may know your success depends on consistently practicing the new habit but have trouble maintaining your enthusiasm over time.

Persistence is continuing to take action even when you are tempted to skip it, just this once. The problem with *just this once* is that it becomes *just this twice* and then *just these three times*, and pretty soon you've stopped doing it altogether.

Achieving challenging goals requires persistence. You must stick with the goal until you achieve it. Stay in the game. Be disciplined. Make taking action like brushing your teeth. Do it whether you feel like it or not, because you know it's good for you. Failing to take care of your health can shorten your life. Failing to take consistent action on your goals can shorten the quality of your life. If an action is needed to achieve the goal, just do it.

Be honest with yourself about whether you're willing to persist until you achieve your goal. Honesty is having the integrity to own your actions and their consequences. It means not making excuses or placing blame elsewhere. It's taking responsibility for what is within your control. You presumably set the goal because achieving it was important to you. Either you want something you don't have, or you don't want something you have. That being the case, you have three options: (1) You can abandon your goal and settle for things as they are. (2) You can keep the goal but abandon your plan and just hope you'll get lucky and things will change without your having to do anything. Or (3) You can continue to take action to achieve your goal until you make it happen. Honesty is telling yourself the truth about which option you choose, which is determined by what you do, not by what you say. If you choose option 3, congratulations and welcome to *The World Series of Thinking*.

Hint #5: Audit how you spend your time.

If you don't feel you are making progress as quickly as you'd like, conduct a time audit of your actions. Lawyers and consultants track their billable hours because that's how they get paid. For them, time is money. You should treat time the same way and track your actions by the hour. You may be surprised at how you spend your days.

Record what you're doing in real time, hour by hour, for at least a week. Using a daily planner will make it easier to do. You may find you are not spending as much time on your goal as you thought. Maybe you're putting off working on your goal until late in the day when you have less energy. Maybe you're getting distracted by other things. Maybe you're wasting time checking emails or social media or killing time in some other way.

Looking at how you spend your time can be eye-opening, and not just relative to your current goal. Imagine what your planner would tell you if you had been recording your actions on an hourly basis for the past month, year, or decade. What have you been doing? Is how you spend your time how you want to be spending it? Is it getting you where you want to go? Your daily allotment of time and energy is limited. Each day ask yourself, How do I choose to spend my time and energy today? And, with whom do I choose to spend it?

If you're spending your time the same way every day out of habit, rather than intention, a time audit can be a wake-up call.

If you continue to track your time and actions going forward, the process will keep you focused. You can use your planner to ensure you are spending your time mindfully rather than mindlessly. Just knowing you are going to have to account for your time will remind you to spend it wisely.

Hint #6: If you get off track, get back on.

Even when you are taking consistent action to achieve a goal, you are likely to get off track sometimes. Distractions happen. Unexpected issues arise. The issues may be directly related to the goal, or they may be unrelated but affect the time and energy you have to work on your goal.

Don't give up if you fall behind in executing your plan. Just reassess where you are at the first available opportunity. For instance, if you find you are a week behind on your plan, use your critical and creative thinking skills to figure out what you need to do to get back on track. Could you combine some tasks? Can you think of a way to do something quicker? Can you cut something out without jeopardizing the goal? Could you cancel something less important to free up more time for your goal? Could you pull in some additional resources to get caught up?

If you think about it, you can find solutions that never occurred to you before. For instance, you may look at your calendar and see appointments, meetings, and activities, and consider that time unavailable. But is it? Are all those scheduled activities necessary? Could a phone call or email take the place of a meeting? Could you save time by ordering online instead of running errands? Are there things you do, or people you spend time with, out of habit rather than desire? Life is about making choices. Make them deliberately, not by default.

The critical thing is not to give up when you get off track. Don't quit; recommit. If your goal is important, it's worth sticking with it. Setbacks are inevitable, but they need not be permanent. If you get off track, get back on.

The action step is where change happens. It is the place where the seeds of success are sown. Goals and plans have the *potential* to change your life, but only action has the *power* to change it. Action is both the riskiest and most rewarding step. And actions speak louder than words…what are yours saying?

Chapter 10:

Step 4: Analyze Your Results

"Life is pretty simple: You do some stuff. Most fails. Some works. You do more of what works. If it works big, others quickly copy it. Then you do something else. The trick is in the doing something else."

—attributed to Leonardo da Vinci (and Tom Peters)

After setting a goal, creating a plan, and taking action, you finally arrive at the last step of the achievement process: analyzing the results. What happened and why did it happen? Most games have three possible outcomes: win, lose, or tie. *The Thinking Game* is similar, but the outcomes are win, learn, or lose. If you achieve your goal, you win. If you try but fail to achieve your goal, you learn. If you quit on the goal altogether, you lose.

As you continue to play *The Thinking Game*, you will accumulate more wins if you analyze your results. Regardless of the outcome, you'll improve your future results if you take time to think through what happened. As Rule #6 states, you will progress more quickly if you learn from your results.

In sports, coaches and players often watch films of their games to analyze what happened. If something worked, why did it work? If something didn't work, why didn't it work? What did they do well? What did they do poorly? How much did the game plan and decisions of the coaches affect the outcome of the game? How much did the effort, skill, preparation, and mindset of the players affect the outcome of the game? How much did luck influence the outcome? Most important, how can the team improve going forward?

A similar review process is used by people in the military and business world, but they call it an after-action report. They analyze what happened and why, so they can build on strengths, counter weaknesses, and improve results going forward.

You can prepare after-action reports to analyze and improve your results. Documenting your results can also help you create a system for achieving similar goals in the future.

Create an after-action report that answers these questions:

1. What was supposed to happen?
2. What actually happened?
3. Why did it happen?
4. What did you learn?
5. What changes will you make as a result of what you learned?

The Thinking Game

By answering these five questions, you can improve your thinking and your results going forward. A major reason that many people don't significantly improve their lives over time is that they don't learn from their successes or failures. If they succeed, they celebrate briefly and move on. Since they don't bother analyzing *why* they succeeded, they can't consciously repeat that success in the future. If they fail, they make excuses, place blame, or console themselves and move on. Since they don't bother analyzing *why* they failed, they can't learn from it or consciously improve future results.

Question #1: What was supposed to happen?

The first question is easy to answer. What was supposed to happen is the achievement of your goal. If you set a goal that was clear, measurable, and time-based, you already know what was supposed to happen.

Question #2: What actually happened?

The second question is also easy to answer if you set a clear goal. What were your results? For instance, if your goal were to finish in the top 100 in this year's Boston Marathon, then your results might be that you came in 90th in this year's Boston Marathon. The clearer your original goal, the easier it is to state your results relative to the goal.

If you set a vague goal, like a goal to improve your productivity, it will be harder to conclusively state your results. The best you could do is state whether you *think* you improved your productivity. Very subjective.

If you cannot clearly state what happened, you may need to spend more time in the future clarifying your goals.

Question #3: Why did it happen?

Now the questions become more difficult. Especially for big goals, your results are likely due to multiple factors. When you are trying to figure out why you got the results you did, keep drilling down. Why did this happen? Why else did this happen?

Before you start your analysis, put yourself in the right frame of mind. If you are emotional, you will have a hard time analyzing why your results happened. If you are still caught up in the excitement of achieving your goal, you are more likely to attribute your success to personal factors like being smart and talented instead of figuring out which plans and actions helped you succeed. It's hard to systematize *smart and talented* for future goals. If you are still upset by a failure, you're more likely to blame others or bad luck, rather than figuring out what really caused your results. You can't learn anything that will help you improve future results if you are not in the mood to consider whether your own faulty plans or actions contributed to your failure. Remember, there's no shame in trying and failing. It's an opportunity to learn.

What is a shame is never trying at all or quitting when you run into obstacles.

When assessing why your results happened, it helps to focus your thoughts on five areas: The Goal, The Plan, The Action, Other People, and Luck. It's advisable to consider the factors in that order because it places the initial emphasis on what *you* control: your goal, your plan, and your actions. Since you have less control over other people and luck, it's to your benefit to consider them last. After all, the ultimate goal is to improve your results, and you can't do that if you focus on things outside your control.

The Goal. The first area to consider when analyzing your results is the goal you set. What you're really trying to determine is whether there were any issues with the goal itself that unduly impacted your results. If you set the goal using the criteria previously discussed, this may be a quick analysis.

If you failed to achieve your goal, was it because the goal was not that important to you? Was it a goal you thought you should achieve, rather than one you wanted to achieve? Was it someone else's goal? If so, your results may reflect the fact that you didn't really care about the goal.

Was the goal reasonable? You can, and should, set stretch goals, but it is possible to stretch too far. If your results improved significantly but you still failed to hit your goal, the goal may have been too big of a stretch. Maybe technically you failed to achieve your goal, but sometimes a loss is really a win. On the other hand, if you set a goal you easily achieved, then you didn't stretch far enough. Achieving goals by sandbagging may fool others, but it won't increase your confidence or help you achieve future success. Maybe technically you achieved your goal, but sometimes a win is really a loss.

Was the goal within your control? If achieving the goal depended more on other people or luck than on your own plans and actions, the goal was not within your control. These types of goals are more hope-based than reality-based. Better to choose goals over which you have significant control if you want to achieve meaningful results.

The primary purpose of analyzing the goal in light of the results is to ensure that there were no flaws with the goal itself. By doing this post-action analysis of the goal, you will get better at setting future goals.

The Plan. The next factor to analyze is the plan. If you effectively executed the plan but didn't get the results you were seeking, this would point to an issue with the plan itself.

One area to evaluate is timing. If you missed the deadline for achieving your goal, compare actual completion dates to scheduled dates for the tasks in your plan. Was the timing too aggressive? Did the plan not allow enough time for distractions, interruptions, or delays? Were there timing issues over which you had no control?

Another area to consider is whether there were issues with any of the specific tasks included in your plan. Were there any tasks that did not help you achieve your goal? For example, in hindsight, were any of the tasks in your plan a waste of time? For instance, if your goal were to grow your business, one of your planned tasks may have been to promote your business using social media advertising. When you review your results, you may find that the advertising was costly and didn't help you grow your business. Continuing to drill down on why certain tasks were not effective can help you with future planning.

Also, consider what wasn't in your plan that should have been. If you tracked your actions against the plan as we discussed, you'd be able to see if you ended up needing to take critical actions that were not included in your plan.

Think about each task in your plan given the hindsight of your results. What worked? What didn't? Ask questions like, Did I include the right tasks? Did I anticipate the challenges I faced? Should I have used more, or different, resources?

By evaluating the strengths and weaknesses of your plan, you'll create better plans going forward.

The Action. Next, analyze your actions. If you documented your actions, you should have a pretty good idea of what actions you took, both planned and unplanned.

For the planned actions you took, try to determine how well you executed them. You will have already thought about whether they were the right actions to take when you analyzed the plan. For the unplanned actions, look at whether they were the right actions to take *and* whether you executed them well. What you're trying to figure out is the effectiveness of your actions.

Of course, your analysis will be subjective. But if you're genuinely looking to improve your results, you can be more objective by analyzing your actions as if they were taken by someone else. Sometimes the effectiveness of your actions will be obvious. For instance, if you applied to get into a school and were accepted, clearly your actions were effective. If you spent a considerable amount of money on a new technology that didn't work out, clearly that action was ineffective.

But many times, determining the effectiveness of your actions will be a gray area. For instance, if you accomplished a task but did it inefficiently, that action was semi-effective. You got it done, but there's room for improvement in your process for doing it.

Now that you know how things turned out, look at each critical action taken and determine how well you think you executed it. If you think you executed it well, you may have uncovered a strength you can build on. If you think your execution could be improved, you may have discovered a weakness you can correct. Do you need to improve a skill? Do you need to put in more effort? Do you need to learn how to do a task more efficiently? Assess whether each action was necessary and how well you think you completed it.

By studying your actions in light of your results, you'll begin to make better connections between actions and consequences. You'll also become more aware of your strengths and weaknesses, which will help you improve future actions. Each time you do this analysis, you'll learn and grow.

Other People. If your goal involved other people, determine how they influenced your results. Focus on how you think other people helped or hurt your efforts to achieve your goal.

When looking at the impact of other people, you are not trying to find someone to blame. You are trying to understand what happened. If you think someone hindered your ability to achieve your goal, question what happened until you feel you've arrived at the truth. Depending on the situation, you may even want to seek feedback from other people. For instance, you may think you missed a deadline because your freelancer didn't get their work to you on time, but they may think your instructions were unclear. Consider both perspectives. Own your part and improve your actions going forward.

It's equally important to consider how other people helped you achieve your goal. We are often more aware of our own contributions than those of others. We unconsciously magnify what we did, but downplay what others did. If someone helped you achieve your goal, acknowledge their contribution. Not only is it the right thing to do, but it also increases the possibility that they'll help you again in the future. Remember, you are trying to figure out why you succeeded in achieving your goal, so you can repeat your success going forward. Success is often a group effort.

Once you're clear on the impact of other people's actions on your results, you'll have a better idea of how to work with the same (or different) people to achieve your future goals. Of course, you'll also want to help them with their goals. If you take, but don't give, you'll soon have no one to take from.

Luck. As indicated by Rule #5 of *The Thinking Game*, luck is a wild card. It sometimes works in your favor and sometimes works against you. Keep that in mind when you're doing your after-action report. Be as honest as you can. This is a good time to refer back to the list of cognitive biases, especially the self-serving bias. When you are analyzing your results, beware of the unconscious tendency to give yourself all the credit for successes but blame failures on bad luck, other people, or other factors.

Make it a point to actively look for where you were lucky and unlucky when you evaluate your results. Ask: Where did I get lucky when working on this goal? For instance, if your neighbor knew an executive at a company where you wanted to work and made a personal introduction, that was good luck. Also ask: Where did I get unlucky? For example, if the value of your investment portfolio declined by the same percentage the market declined, then bad luck contributed to your results. When bad luck occurs, think about how you might guard against similar bad luck in the future. For instance, in the prior example, you might want to research strategies for hedging against market downturns.

In addition to looking at where you got lucky or unlucky, analyze how you handled your luck. Did you take full advantage of lucky breaks? Did you handle bad luck as best you could and move on, or did you dwell on it?

It's important to determine how luck affected your results. If you underemphasize the impact of good luck, it can cause you to be overconfident of your skills, to your future detriment. If you overemphasize the impact of bad luck, you may fail to improve your plans and actions, also to your future detriment. Luck should be put in its proper perspective. Good luck with that.

Question #4: What did you learn?

For this part of your after-action report, the objective is to determine key lessons learned. What were the most important things you learned as a result of analyzing your results?

Focus on the bigger picture. You want to primarily look for information that will help you in the future. For instance, if your analysis revealed that being disorganized caused you to miss deadlines, that would be a key lesson learned. If you discovered that a new freelancer provided high-quality service, that would be a key lesson learned and a good future resource. If your analysis showed that a chronic problem you had never fully addressed impeded your ability to achieve your goal, that would be a key lesson learned. You get the idea.

Be as specific as possible. Vague lessons are about as helpful as vague goals. If your lesson learned is that you need to work harder, that isn't very actionable. Clarity is key. If what you really mean is that you learned the reason you could not get your work done during normal office hours is that you spend up to 2 hours a day socializing with co-workers, then say that. That's actionable.

Look for patterns. If your analysis showed that you were resourceful in numerous instances when faced with constraints, that's a pattern...and a good one. If your analysis showed that every time you ran into an unexpected challenge, you fell apart and someone else had to bail you out, that's a pattern...but a bad one. Patterns can help you discover strengths, weaknesses, opportunities, and threats. Pattern-finding is particularly effective for uncovering chronic issues. If you can identify and correct ongoing issues that hinder your success, you can significantly improve your results in a shorter amount of time.

Success and satisfaction are not one-offs. They are the cumulative effect of thoughts and actions over time. So when you consider what you learned in achieving any *one* goal, also think about how it can help you achieve *all* goals. If you continue to apply what you learn, you'll make significantly quicker progress in life.

Question #5: What changes will you make as a result of what you learned?

Awareness without action is useless. To finalize your after-action report, you must decide what to do with what you've learned. What changes will you make?

The changes you make will obviously depend on what you learned when you analyzed your results. For instance, if you learned you waste too much time during the day checking emails or social media, you might decide to limit those activities to 30 minutes a day. If you learned that people responded well to a business presentation you gave, you might decide to look for additional public speaking opportunities.

As a result of each lesson you learned, ask yourself:

1. What will I change? (New Goal)
2. How will I change it? (New Plan)

If you're not clear on what you need to do as a result of what you've learned, ask yourself questions to gain clarification. For instance, you might ask yourself:

- Do I need to change how I think or feel about this issue?
- Do I need to change a habit to improve future results?
- Do I need to change how I spend my time?
- Do I need to change any personal or professional relationships?
- Do I need to change how I approach problems?
- Do I need to create or change a system or process?
- Is there anything else I need to change based on what I've learned?

Continue to ask questions until you've clarified what you need to change and then create a plan for changing it.

The process for achieving goals is circular. You set the goal, then create the plan, then take action, and then analyze the results. Based on what you learn, you set another goal, create another plan...and so on, continuing the same four steps. You just connect four steps and repeat the process with each new goal, taking breaks in between goals to rest and recharge. The four-step process is how you apply what you learn and create even greater success in the future.

By continuing to create written after-action reports for major goals, you'll build a personal knowledge base you can use to address future goals. In effect, you'll create your own systems and best practices. Why start over each time you set a new goal? Build on what you've learned from past experience.

The after-action reports don't have to be lengthy. For some goals, you may only need a page or two. You can even create a template to guide your analysis. Create a document with the title "After-Action Report" for XYZ goal and include the 5 questions:

1. What was supposed to happen?
2. What actually happened?
3. Why did it happen?
4. What did I learn?
5. What changes will I make as a result of what I learned?

Then for each important goal you set, pull out the template and answer the questions to help you analyze your results. If you keep asking questions, you'll keep finding answers.

As long as you push through on your goals, the outcome is not win or lose, it's win or learn. Winning feels good, and if you keep using the 4-step process for achieving goals, you'll get more wins. But no one wins every time. When you fall short of a goal, learn from the experience and apply it to your future efforts. The only way to lose *The Thinking Game* is to quit. So don't.

Conclusion:

Take Your Thinking Game to New Heights

"From right understanding proceeds right thought; from right thought proceeds right speech; from right speech proceeds right action; from right action proceeds right livelihood; from right livelihood proceeds right effort; from right effort proceeds right awareness; from right awareness proceeds right concentration; from right concentration proceeds right wisdom; from right wisdom proceeds right liberation."

—attributed to Buddha

The object of *The Thinking Game* is to achieve a goal chosen by you. You accomplish this objective by using the four-step achievement process of setting the right goal, creating the right plan, taking the right action, and analyzing your results. All four steps require asking and answering questions.

Questioning is the essence of thinking. Ask questions, and you will receive answers. Ask better questions, and you will receive better answers. By practicing the thinking mindset, skills, and techniques discussed in this guide, you will unquestionably become a more effective thinker.

Conscious thinking gives you focus and allows you to assume control over the direction of your life. You have the right to set your own goals. If you give up this right, your goals will be set for you by other people and your environment. You can decide from this point forward, Who will choose your goals? You? Other people? Or Fate?

Your unconscious mind can help you achieve success and satisfaction if your conscious mind provides clear directions. If you don't provide direction, your unconscious mind will simply recreate your past in your present. You will react automatically to current situations based on the thoughts and feelings triggered by similar past experiences. If you consciously object to unhelpful thoughts by replacing them with helpful thoughts, your unconscious mind will overrule you at first. But if you persist, your unconscious will eventually sustain your new way of thinking. Your new thoughts, feelings, and actions will then take precedence over your old ones. That is how you train your unconscious mind to support your new way of thinking. One thought at a time. One day at a time.

Time and energy are limited when you think of them in daily increments. But when you string together the days, weeks, months, and years of your life, the amount of time and energy you have is practically unlimited. You have time to play *The Thinking Game* and achieve your goals.

The rules of *The Thinking Game* are simple:

1. The object of *The Thinking Game* is to achieve a goal.
2. You play the game with others but only control your own moves.
3. You can play or pass but there are consequences to your actions.
4. Greater goals require greater time and effort.
5. Luck is a wild card which can work for you or against you.
6. You will progress more quickly if you learn from your results.
7. You win by mastering your conscious mind and managing your unconscious mind.

If you remember the rules, you'll rack up more wins in the game. The rules are reality based, and reality always wins in the end. Fighting the rules is tempting. We *want* to control what other people do. We *don't want* to work harder to achieve challenging goals. But, alas, reality is what it is. Embrace it, and you'll swim with life's current instead of struggling against it.

Your life is what you think it is. Change your thoughts, change your life. Keep the thoughts you have, keep the life you have. It's that simple, but simple doesn't mean easy. Easy is boring, and you must sacrifice boredom if you want a satisfying life. The things you value most are those you work hardest for, not those that come easily to you. Thinking is hard. Because of that, most people avoid conscious thinking. As Bertrand Russell noted, "Many people would sooner die than think; in fact, they do." But many people are also unhappy. Coincidence?

Like any other skill, thinking improves and becomes easier the more you consciously do it. Consider all the things you make time for in your life. Where is thinking on your list? Make it a priority. Schedule thinking time on your calendar. When you start exercising your body, you start slowly and build from there. To start exercising your mind, start slowly and build from there. A few minutes a day, an hour a week, one day a month, one week a year. When you begin to see changes in how you feel and what you're able to accomplish, you'll naturally increase your thinking time. Taking time to think will become a habit. Your unconscious mind will prod your conscious mind to do it.

Life is like a labyrinth: there's only one path into it and one path out of it. But in between those two points, your life is like a maze. As you experiment and try things, you'll make some good moves, but you'll also run into some dead ends. If you consciously think about your experiences and learn from them, you won't have to go down the same dead-end roads more than once or twice. You can improve your sense of direction and reach your goals more quickly. Learn to love the journey, not just the destination.

Own who you are and what you think, and your path forward will become clearer.

Thinking is our greatest power. It is our ticket to ride in life. Thinking allows us to evolve intentionally, rather than accidentally. It enables us to control our actions and influence our results. It is how we learn and create. It brings clarity out of chaos. It is how we know ourselves. It is the path to fulfillment, success, and happiness. It is the only way to change the world for the better. And, as William Shakespeare said, "Thought is free." Anyone can afford to think, no one can afford not to.

The Thinking Game can be played again and again with different goals. The game never ends. The ultimate goal is a successful and satisfying life, and you can build that life one goal at a time. What matters most is not the individual goals you choose, but who you become in the process of achieving them.

What goes on in your head determines how you experience life, so it pays to master *The Thinking Game*. It is challenging, rewarding, and fun to keep improving how you play the game. Who knows what you can achieve and become. You will have to push yourself out of your comfort zone, but that's a small price to pay for a fulfilling life. *Don't you think?*

Appendix:

Selected Bibliography – 50 Thought-Provoking Books

Below is an alphabetical list of my favorite books on thinking, which I consulted in the course of writing *The Thinking Game*. The complete list of books I've read about thinking is longer, but I omitted any books that I wouldn't recommend to a friend.

The information provided includes the title and subtitle, the author(s), and the year the book was originally published. I didn't include the name of the publisher because the publisher of a book sometimes changes. Authors may use a different publisher for reprints, different formats, or revised editions. Additionally, in the United States, books published more than 95 years ago become public domain books, which means they are no longer protected by copyright. Once that happens, anyone can publish the book, which is why you'll often see numerous publishers for ancient classics like the Tao te Ching.

1. ***As a Man Thinketh***. James Allen. 1903.
2. ***Awareness***. Anthony de Mello. 1990.

3. *Blink: The Power of Thinking Without Thinking.*
   Malcolm Gladwell. 2005.

4. *Brain Rules: 12 Principles for Surviving and Thriving at Work, Home, and School.* John Medina. 2008.

5. *Buddhism Plain and Simple: The Practice of Being Aware, Right Now, Every Day.* Steve Hagen. 1997.

6. *Calm Clarity: How to Use Science to Rewire Your Brain for Greater Wisdom, Fulfillment, and Joy.* Due Quach. 2018.

7. *Essentialism: The Disciplined Pursuit of Less.* Greg McKeown. 2011.

8. *Executive Toughness: The Mental-Training Program to Increase Your Leadership Performance.* Dr. Jason Selk. 2011.

9. *Factfulness: Ten Reasons We're Wrong about the World – and Why Things are Better Than You Think.* Hans Rosling with Ola Rosling and Anna Rosling Rönnlund. 2018.

10. *Hit Makers: How to Succeed in an Age of Distraction.* Derek Thompson. 2017.

11. *How to Fly a Horse: The Secret History of Creation, Invention, and Discovery.* Kevin Ashton. 2015.

12. *How to Think: A Survival Guide for a World at Odds.* Alan Jacobs. 2017.

13. *Idiot Brain: What Your Head is Really Up To*. Dean Burnett. 2016.

14. *Meditations*. Marcus Aurelius. Written circa 167 A.C.E. and originally published in 1558.

15. *Mind Power into the 21ˢᵗ Century.* John Kehoe. 1987.

16. *Mindset: The New Psychology of Success*. Carol S. Dweck. 2006.

17. *Mindwise: Why We Misunderstand What Others Think, Believe, Feel, and Want*. Nicholas Epley. 2014.

18. *Nudge: Improving Decisions About Health, Wealth, and Happiness*. Richard H. Thaler and Cass R. Sunstein. 2008.

19. *On Human Nature*. Edward O. Wilson. 1978.

20. *Predictably Irrational: The Hidden Forces that Shape Our Decisions*. Dan Ariely. 2008.

21. *Principles: Life and Work*. Ray Dalio. 2017.

22. *Problem Solving 101: A Simple Book for Smart People*. Ken Watanabe. 2009.

23. *Six Thinking Hats*. Edward de Bono. 1985.

24. *Strangers to Ourselves: Discovering the Adaptive Unconscious*. Timothy D. Wilson. 2002.

25. *Tao te Ching*. Lao Tzu (Laozi). Circa 4ᵀᴴ Century B.C.E. (Stephen Mitchell translation - 2006).

26. *The 5 Elements of Effective Thinking*. Edward B. Burger and Michael Starbird. 2012.

27. *The 7 Habits of Highly Effective People: Powerful Lessons in Personal Change*. Stephen Covey. 1989.

28. *The Art of Thinking Clearly*. Rolf Dobelli. 2011.

29. *The Art of Worldly Wisdom*. Baltasar Gracián. 1647.

30. *The Autobiography of Benjamin Franklin*. Benjamin Franklin. 1791.

31. *The Brain: The Story of You*. David Eagleman. 2015.

32. *The Code of the Extraordinary Mind: 10 Unconventional Laws to Redefine Your Life and Succeed on Your Own Terms*. Vishen Lakhiani. 2016.

33. *The Compound Effect: Jumpstart Your Income, Your Life, Your Success*. Darren Hardy. 2010.

34. *The Consciousness Instinct: Unraveling the Mystery of How the Brain Makes Your Mind*. Michael S. Gazzaniga. 2018.

35. *The Laws of Human Nature*. Robert Greene. 2018.

36. *The Power of Your Subconscious Mind*. Dr. Joseph Murphy. 1962.

37. *The Science of Mind*. Ernest Holmes. 1926.

38. *The Seven Decisions: Understanding the Keys to Personal Success*. Andy Andrews. 2014.

39. *The Thinking Life: How to Thrive in the Age of Distractions*. P. M. Forni. 2011.

40. *The Tipping Point: How Little Things Can Make a Big Difference*. Malcolm Gladwell. 2000.

41. ***The Ultimate Secrets of Total Self-Confidence.*** Dr. Robert Anthony. 1979.

42. ***The War of Art: Break Through the Blocks and Win Your Inner Creative Battles.*** Steven Pressfield. 2002.

43. ***Think and Grow Rich.*** Napoleon Hill. 1937.

44. ***Think Smarter: Critical Thinking to Improve Problem-Solving and Decision-Making Skills.*** Michael Kallet. 2014.

45. ***Thinking in Bets: Making Smarter Decisions When You Don't Have All the Facts.*** Annie Duke. 2018.

46. ***Thinking, Fast and Slow.*** Daniel Kahneman. 2011.

47. ***Thinking: The New Science of Decision-Making, Problem-Solving, and Prediction.*** Edited by John Brockman (with contributions from Daniel Kahneman, Jonathan Haidt, Daniel C. Dennett, Nassim Nicholas Taleb, and more). 2013.

48. ***Understanding Human Nature.*** Alfred Adler. 1927.

49. ***What to Say When You Talk to Your Self.*** Shad Helmstetter, Ph.D. 1986.

50. ***You Are Not Your Brain: The 4-Step Solution for Changing Bad Habits, Ending Unhealthy Thinking, and Taking Control of Your Life.*** Jeffrey M. Schwartz, M.D. and Rebecca Gladding, M.D. 2011.

If you have a favorite thought-provoking book that's not on the list, please email me the title at kara@karalanc.com.

Acknowledgments

"I can no more remember the books I have read than the meals I have eaten, but they have made me."

—attributed to Ralph Waldo Emerson

It's impossible for an author to thank everyone who contributed to a book because we are influenced by all the books we've read before, including those long forgotten. I don't remember the title of every good book I've read, but I wish to thank all the authors who have contributed to how, and what, I think.

In addition to thanking the authors recognized in the Appendix, I want to thank Jessica Filippi for critiquing and formatting *The Thinking Game*, Meella at 99designs for designing the book's cover, and the beta readers who provided feedback on my manuscript prior to publication. I also want to thank Jane Friedman for critiquing my website and blog, Christina Katz for providing branding insights, and Matthew Doudt for creating my author photos.

I am also grateful for the online resources that verify quotes, such as Wikiquote, Quote Investigator, and Google Books. And I appreciate the timely advice in *Dryer's English* from Random House copy chief Benjamin Dryer who encourages us to split infinitives, end sentences with prepositions, and begin sentences with "And" or "But" if it helps us communicate clearly with readers. Rules are made to be broken and writing, like thinking, should continue to evolve.

Finally, I want to thank my husband, Rick. Not only did he provide valuable input as a beta reader for *The Thinking Game*, but he also supported me through the long hours I spent writing, editing, and fretting about it. I am lucky and forever grateful for who he is and all that he does.

About the Author

Kara Lane has published multiple books on various subjects. The common thread in all her books is that she "cracked the code" on how to do something better – from creating a better wardrobe to living a better life. In addition to *The Thinking* **Game**, she has written the following books:

- **The Smart Woman's Guide to Style & Clothing**
  A Step-By-Step Process for Creating the Perfect Wardrobe

- **From Photographer to Gallery Artist**
  The Complete Guide to Finding Gallery Representation for Your Fine Art Photography

- **Simoni's Gift**
  A Story about Your Purpose in Life

- **Wake Up to Powerful Living**
  12 Principles to Transform Your Life!

Contact Information:
Website: www.karalane.com
Email: kara@karalane.com
Twitter: @AuthorKaraLane

In addition to writing books, Kara Lane is a Certified Public Accountant (CPA), a Certified Professional Coach, and a public speaker. She grew up in Indianapolis and received her Bachelor of Science degree in Business from Indiana University, where she graduated with Highest Distinction. She currently lives in Carmel, Indiana, with her husband, Rick Lane.

P.S. If you enjoyed reading *The Thinking Game*, please leave a review for other readers on the website of the bookseller from whom you purchased the book.

"Books allow you to fully explore a topic and immerse yourself in a deeper way than most media today. I'm looking forward to shifting more of my media diet towards reading books."
—Mark Zuckerberg (2015)

"You don't have to burn books to destroy a culture. Just get people to stop reading them."
—Ray Bradbury (1993)

"No one ever reads a book. He reads himself through books, either to discover or to control himself."
—Romain Rolland (1947)

"You will get little or nothing from the printed page if you bring it nothing but your eye."
—Walter Pitkin (1930)

"Tis the good reader that makes the good book; in every book he finds passages which seem confidences or asides hidden from all else and unmistakenly meant for his ear."
—Ralph Waldo Emerson (1870)

Thank you for reading *The Thinking Game*.
I hope you found the hidden messages meant for you alone.

www.ingramcontent.com/pod-product-compliance
Lightning Source LLC
Chambersburg PA
CBHW031933090426
42811CB00002B/169